THE LIBERATORS

The further accounts and experiences of the author of *The Strongest Weapon* — NOTBURGA TILT.

When the war ended, she was barely twenty-two years old and decided to continue her singing career, interrupted by her joining the Austrian Widerstand — Resistance Movement.

NOW it was 1946, now or never for the young girl, who had already sacrificed five years of her life, fighting on behalf of freedom for mankind, to secure a place in the sun, in her beloved city Vienna, once the metropolis of the musical world and imperial splendour.

Nothing was going to stand in her way of success and indeed, she was lucky and supported by very influential relatives . . . friends and high-ranking Allied officers.

The latter however, desired her sensual beauty and youth more than her talents, as an artist and Notburga had to choose . . . . . between morality and hunger.

Did she lead a life of excess — or was she the sad victim of circumstances? It is up to the reader to judge.

This is truly a portrait of a soul, where corruption and the Black Market dictated the pulse of a city and its people.

By the same author:
The Strongest Weapon

THE LIBERATORS

Notburga Tilt

ARTHUR H. STOCKWELL LTD.
Elms Court   Ilfracombe
Devon

ISBN 0 7223 2511-8
Printed in Great Britain by
Arthur H. Stockwell Ltd.
Elms Court   Ilfracombe
Devon

Contents

Illustration page 169
British Transit Hotel, Astoria

page 170—172 — *Love-letter from Major Kornelius de Kuypers, who served with the British Army and had a suite at the Hotel Astoria*

page 173—174 — *Business contracts involving large amounts of money signed and approved by Captain M. Spreckley, Manager of the Hotel Astoria, with him retaining the* ENGLISH *translation*

page 175 — *Post-card from 'KAMILLA', the Hotel Receptionist from a holiday resort, with her boy-friend, the British Colonel . . . and BEFORE her revelation to me of my PAST as an SS-guard in Poland . . . ORIGINAL card (authentic) — readable and signed*

page 175 — *Visiting card of Herr Erich Zartl, well-known Casino and Cafe owner, left with Mrs Ell, plus large amounts of* English currency

page 176 — *Letter from General de Gaulle, confirming the author's involvement with the French Resistance, as a courier*

page 176 — *Letter to the, then Mrs Burgi Ell, from Captain M. Spreckley, tracing her to Newmarket, England*

The Author

Foreword — By Kay Heriot
former editor of *Time* magazine, New York

In the Spring of 1940, after the fall of France, England's greatest representative and spokesman for the free world, Sir Winston Churchill, said: "All over Europe the lights have gone out . . . " In the Spring of 1945, the Allied victors, surrounded by the ghosts of the millions who had died for Freedom, switched them on again.

The authoress of this book had managed to stay alive. Yet during the five years of her activities as a deeply committed member of the Austrian Resistance she had endured the tortures of the Gestapo and, one might say, really outlived the nine lives of a cat. She was only twenty-two years old (or should one say, young?), when she confronted the Liberators — not, it must be emphasized, as part of the spoils of war, but as a fighter in her own right, demanding justice and the opportunity to pursue her own career as a singer in Vienna, once the music capital of the world.

She was a highly talented, vibrant and beautiful girl, inspired by passion and uncommonly deep feelings herself, and she inspired an overpowering infatuation and love in some very powerful men, and something shuddered within them at the actuality of the events that followed.

Was it the height of the Seventh Heaven, or a kind of capitulation on both sides, with the WOMAN holding the key with which to unlock and penetrate the secrets of the heart?

A fascinating problem, which even those who have the pleasure and the privilege to have known the authoress for a long time will never really cease to ponder over. She is a truly unique lady and one of the few, whose shoulders did hold the sky suspended, when earth's foundations seemed to shake to a much more frightening extent than the poet A. E. Housman could have imagined them shaking decades earlier, when he wrote his epitaph on the Army of Mercenaries, who had to contend with much less horror than those who fought the Gestapo — and *not* as mercenaries! We all owe our thanks to the authoress of this book.

Kay Heriot
B.A., M.A., Ph.D.

Introduction

My name is Notburga Theresia Agnes Tilt, Baroness von Haan. The way by which I came to have the title and rather unusual names, must have been the prelude to my exciting life. I have searched and exposed my very soul to write this true story of my own life, in which a little convent girl from Graz — Austria became a Resistance fighter, who matured into a 'Femme Fatal', not by choice, but what I believed to be my destiny.

I was born in Graz on the 21st of January 1923, of cosmopolitan parents. My father was Austrian and he served as an officer with the Austrian-Hungarian Army until 1918, and was highly decorated. My mother was Austrian-Czechoslovakian and the only child of a solicitor. We lived in Graz until 1936, and I was educated at the Sacred Heart Convent, considered to be the best and most exclusive in Steiermark. My father died in March 1936 of cancer, a loss that lay heavy on my heart.

In 1938, after the 'Anschluss' in which Hitler made Austria part of the Third Reich, the convent was closed and my education cut short. In 1940, my mother re-married — a bachelor of fifty years of age, and I soon found out all he wanted was a housekeeper, and an animosity between myself and my stepfather developed.

When war broke out in 1939, my family were strongly opposed to Hitler and blacklisted, thus I decided to take up the fight against the Nazis and their terror regime, regardless of the consequences. To me, the German occupation of Austria was a Rape of Liberty, and I was determined, if need be, to sacrifice my young life on the altar of freedom on behalf of the individual, and the benefit of humanity.

Therefore, I dedicate my book to the entire Austrian Widerstand-Resistance and in particular to my most loyal friends, who experienced with me, the unspeakable tortures and hardships. I truly believe our fight must never have been in vain and the brave and complacent reminded of the gigantic struggle to win over evil, or all of Europe would have been filled with extermination camps and terror.

I finally salute the British Forces on land, sea and in the air, for their bravery, and the British people who stood alone for three years like a rock of defiance against a ruthless enemy and won a victory, that will go into history forever.

March 1945. St. Stefan — Austria

The calendar of war was still unfolding and the attitude of most Nazis was they may as well be hung for a sheep as a lamb and go on killing their foes, mainly people in the 'Widerstand', known to the French, as the Resistance movement! My stepfather, who was in charge of over one hundred Wehrmacht's horses had British and French POWs to help him and we all got on very well, although it was strictly forbidden to talk to the prisoners, only on duty. My mother, who defied such orders, often gave the men warm food, cutting down on our already pitiful ration, which got her husband into a rage.

Somehow, my home-life was wretched and only the daily visits from my friend, Major Hans Schoepf, who was the 'Flack Commander', stationed at St. Stefan, lifted the gloomy picture by bringing us food and bottles of wine. Of course, by now with the Royal Air Force flying within feet of his guns, HIS target was not the daredevil pilots, but the 5ft 2ins, curvacious dark-haired girl of twenty — I. Bewitched and bewildered was he, so much so, that I was able to fully function within my own Resistance group, which was now operating in Donawitz at the Iron and Steel Works, blowing up installations, putting their spanners in Hitler's last war efforts.

My own little game with Major Schoepf was greatly appreciated, thus making sure that his men did not get heroic, looking for the enemy; I for one, who was too close to be seen, in particular, with the love-light blinding his vision.

To top it all, my stepfather was watching me and my mother, who was far from well, having sustained an injury from grenade splinters, whilst trying to save the lives, of two young children. Most people in the village respected my mother for her bravery, yet her husband called her action silly and unnecessary, for which I

11

detested him. However, I had little option, but to live under his roof and try to keep the peace.

Rumours went around, that young soldiers were hanging from trees with notes on their bodies — "I am a coward", and when I mentioned it to Major Schoepf (who in civilian life was a solicitor in Munich) he replied, that justice was done. My orders however, were to stay alive and to find out military details, troop movements via my valuable contact, who showered me with favours and everything else he could lay hands on in his unit; but alas, he wanted much more sexual access, at which I was a past master in excuses.

In a strange way, Major Schoepf's romantic outbursts were like music in my ears. I who had to forsake the physical pleasures of love-making, as it was taboo in our group to form liaisons, as one could not be truly in love, and logical at the same time, or so our Resistance 'Ten Commandments' stated.

At the other end of the Nazi ideology, I could see the funny side of the major's outburst, telling me that we will breed a master race and that I was to be that last and only girl to press my heavenly body against his Fuehrer's uniform. Indeed, it needed all my acting ability not to burst out in laughter and tell him what I thought of it.

Although, I lived on a razor's edge, my days and nights were filled with excitement, keeping up the contact with my partisans in the hills, already in paramilitary uniforms, whilst the atrocities of innocent people being shot, in particular for hiding British POWs, reminded me to be extra careful. My head however, could only think of one word, Victory, as promised by Prime Minister Churchill, will be ours and that we shall walk in Majesty. What I needed was the patience of a saint, which I did not have; only discipline and courage, plus the acting ability to convince Schoepf that I was his, after this war was over, thus keeping him in a constant daze, distracting from his orders, to send his soldiers, where I knew my Resistance comrades were fighting and hiding. What a colossal task, but there was no alternative for me in this dangerous situation, and my mother's views were even stronger. "You are playing Russian roulette, my girl, never knowing when the bullet will kill you."

She was right, but it was now or never, or to be, or not to be, that was the question! As the fighting came closer to our village, one could hear the big guns thunder and my 'Flack-hero' Major Schoepf decided to put as many miles as possible between him and personal danger, and he informed me of his move to Linz, near Vienna.

It was like jumping from the frying-pan into the fire, with the

Russian army closing in on the capital, yet Schoepf still hoped for a miracle via his Fuehrer.

"You are coming with me, I cannot possibly leave you here" he said masterfully, but I reminded him, that my mother, will need me more.

The major was adamant, with my stepfather in agreement, to get me out of his way, so I was between the devil and the deep blue sea, and one word from the latter, and my fate was sealed. I had to climb this last hurdle, or perish in the last days of the war, which to me, was unthinkable.

I went into our little chapel and prayed, lighting a candle. The Madonna and Jesus seemed to look down at me, or was I imagining it, as I prayed earnestly:

"Please Holy Mary, give me the courage to face the last ordeals of this awful war, take care of my mother whilst I am away and make the Liberators come faster, to save us from further destruction and killings. I beseech you, if you are the mother of God, then you must hear my pleas as a woman. Don't forsake me now. Amen!"

I kneeled much longer than I intended, expecting a sign from this stone figure smiling sweetly at me . . . 'pull yourself together' . . . I thought, but in times of crisis like these, one earnestly hopes to be saved by a miracle, and I was no exception. Somehow, I left this place of worship much more relaxed and in the hope, that all will be well; when Major Schoepf drove up in his car and halted, asking me, IF I also prayed for him?

"Of course," I said untruthfully, but he jumped from the vehicle and walked with me home; and rather odd, I had the guts to ask him, what would he do IF I told him, that I was in the Resistance? There was a long pause and he replied, turning me towards him, "The only place, I should like to torture you, is in bed Burgi, does this answer your question?"

I began walking faster, as if trying to escape from his holding me by the waist; but where to? Could I run now, after I had burnt all my bridges behind me? Although Schoepf was talking his usual sexy rubbish to me, my mind was towards the liberation, and I wanted to feel the arms of a British soldier holding me tightly shouting; "It's all over now, we've won . . we've won, you and I are the victors."

The major looked at me as if he had just seen a new woman, my head held high defiantly squaring up to him; but soon I realised, that the time was not right to challenge his superiority, and I had to change my tactics, changing into being his frightened depending girl-friend. 'The loving' look, so often practised removed the pride in my eyes, as he bent over to kiss me in the middle of the street, exclaiming, "I only have to be near you, and I am falling to pieces Burgi."

Capitulation, I thought, one way or the other, lifting my spirit just that bit higher and taking the pressure off my tortured mind.

We said "Auf Wiedersehen," until the evening and I hurried back to my home, which was a bungalow-type of house divided into three flats, and we occupied five rooms, with my own window facing the large stables and beautiful horses galloping free in the grounds. Often I wished that one would take me away, as long as his legs would last, over the mountains and into nearby Switzerland and freedom; but this was only a pipe-dream.

It was now March the 31st, cold and dismal, with heavy snow falling and the country transformed into a fairyland, with the ogres still among us. Sleep, I so much desired became a novelty, and I slept in my jodhpurs, with boots at the ready and my beloved Luger, replacing my heart, but hopefully not for much longer? At 4 a.m., strange noises could be heard coming from the stables. Was it an ambush? I wondered, and dressed in a hurry, checking my revolver and ammunition, just in case. I glanced through the shutters of my window, with cold sweat on my forehead; I simply had to find out what was going on. Be decisive, tough, I thought. This was no film-set, but real action-filled reality, as I crept out of the door, along the fence, with the snow cushioning my footsteps, yet leaving also imprints; but turning back was too late. The light in the bedroom of my parents went on and, IF my stepfather came outside, I was in deep trouble. Thankfully, the light went out again and I proceeded with my investigation, opening the stable door, which squeaked like mad. The horses sensed it was I, and my mare reared up . . . damn it . . . only the Luger in my hand gave me the guts to walk further along the wooden floor. I saw movements by the straw bundles, or did I imagine it . . . my heart was in my mouth, yet I simply could not retreat. I had to move forwards to find out, whatever the cost. I stumbled . . . someone grabbed my feet, and a gloved hand went over my eyes, pushing me to the ground and I felt my Luger taken away from me, in a flash a man's voice said, "We are British POWs from Kraubart Camp, on the run."

"Thank God, I thought you were German deserters," I answered trying to sound brave . . . and the men laughed, obviously at the implication, and the tension was over, as I knew the Kraubart POWs well, not by names of course, but having seen them marching to work. I also told them that I was in the Austrian

Resistance and fought with the partisans in Jugoslavia, to which one of the men replied, "Blimey Jock, this little girl could have shot us by mistake."

Now we all had a good laugh and I asked them, what they wanted of me.

"An old jacket, or coat and something to eat. We are flaming hungry by now, having escaped, three days ago."

I promised to help, if they let go of me, but they retained my gun to make sure that I came back. I hurried into the house and picked up some bread, cheese and a few apples, stuffing them under my sweater. Back in the stables, I found my stepfather's old jacket and the Polish POW's as well, and gave them to my English prisoners, who were delighted, clowning about; but I only wished, they would eat and get going.

Jock was a cheeky fellow, and as if time was of no concern, held my Luger towards his friend, and jokingly said, "It's amazing, what confidence a gun can give you mate."

I urged them to eat what I brought and leave, pointing out (they spoke German) an escape-route via the mountains, plus the name of a farmer they could trust and hide with. They gave me their uniform jackets and told me to burn them, as soon as possible . . . it sounded too proper under normal circumstances, but with the Gestapo breathing down my neck, the penalty for what I was doing, was death by hanging, and certain torture beforehand — still I was prepared to take this risk and Jock kept banging me on the back saying, "Cheer-up girl, the war is over soon," and in turn they hugged me and I told them, also I should like to escape from here, until I could hear the bells of peace sounding.

I opened the back door leading towards the wood. They now had changed their clothes and looked like farm workers, thus standing a fair chance of getting away, and hiding at the next farm, and I wished them luck. Jock handed me back my Luger and jokingly said, "Careful Fräulein, it may go off," and dashed past me saluting.

I crossed myself, and ran back to my bedroom with their uniform jackets under my arm; one was an RAF-blue, the other brown, like the British Army were wearing. My brain was working overtime, how to dispose of the vital evidence before my stepfather got up? I could hear noises from next to my room, my mother's kitchen, and she was obviously in trouble by the sound of it, as her husband kept shouting, and I heard the word 'Burgi', indeed, he only needed to hear me sneeze and accused me of having a man in my room. I braced myself for the worst, as the gravity of my involvement truly hit me and my mother appeared, bringing me some coffee, asking WHY, I was up so early?

"We ought to do our weekly washing before the usual air alarm around 11 a.m.," I said with downcast eyes, plus suggesting to get some paraffin to make the wet wood burn. Mother glanced at me suspiciously, but agreed, and off we marched into the wash-kitchen, which was a small outbuilding close to our house.

As I could feel her eyes on every move I made, I told her that I could manage on my own, and thankfully she decided to leave me filling the large copper vessel with snow, as the water had been turned off for some time.

I sneaked back into my bedroom to fetch the uniform jackets and soaked them with the paraffin, pushing both into the already lit furnace. The explosive liquid sent blue flames against me, sending me reeling backwards, and when my mother entered, she asked, IF I wanted to set the place on fire?

Not a bad idea, I thought and smiled, but she was not amused and it suddenly dawned on her that I was up to something, and she noticed part of the burning jacket. The game was up and all my explanations of what had happened early this morning fell on deaf ears and she raved at me, "How dare you involve us, with the escape of British POWs. They'll hang us, IF we get caught" and she cried, "Have you lost every ounce of common sense my girl?"

There was nothing else I could add or say in my defence, only to urge her to help me burn the damning evidence, as quickly as possible, and alas, she agreed, still shaking like a leaf.

Smoke was billowing over our heads, and our faces got more and more dirty and being me, I could see the funny side of it, and I told mother that also I gave away her husband's old coat and the Pole's jacket.

"For this alone, he will shoot you" she said. Yet it did not bring out the fear in me she expected, and all I could see, were two now black-faced women burning the last rags like fury and to her horror, I teasingly asked, "Just think, what Charlie Chaplin would give for a plot like this?"

Suddenly, we both laughed, she despairing at my sense of humour, but I never accepted defeat in the past five years in the Resistance and the oddest plights, I was involved in. As if all the drama was not enough, we noticed two SS men coming up our path, talking to the Polish POW, then proceeding towards us. My heart missed a beat, yet they laughed, obviously seeing us, black as the ace of spades.

"Have you seen British POWs in this area?"

"Of course not," was our joint reply, "we are too busy with our chores," when to my utter horror, I saw an RAF button which had fallen out of the furnace and nestled in the ashes under my feet. "Don't panic," my brain said, and I moved past the SS soldier, removing my sweater slowly, like in a strip-tease, praying that his eyes will be scrutinizing my body and not the floor.

"It has to be washed," I explained to the still in-a-daze young man.

"We shall call in the evening," was his swift answer, "when you are not so sooty, and have a little fun." They departed laughing down the road.

My mother was flabbergasted when I told her WHY I exposed myself, but soon the stark reality made sense, and she could not see any solution to it all.

"Major Schoepf will save us," I insisted.

But my mother was doubtful and said "You always think of an answer, you clever Dick, but this time you have exhausted your repertoire of excuses," and she was about to enlarge on what was in store for me, when my stepfather entered, demanding to know, where his working coat was, adding, "Also the Pole's jacket has vanished into thin air" and he glared at me.

Mother suggested that we get on with our washing and less talking, as we could hear the heavy bombers in the distance above us, when her husband picked up a piece of burning material, holding it under my nose, shouting at me, "In the house with you my girl, you have gone just too far this time, with my patience," and he pushed me along swearing and cursing my mother and I.

Once inside, he flung me to the other end of the kitchen and my head hit the hard corner of the table. I begged him to listen to reason, but of no avail, and he was beside himself with rage. My mother pleaded for mercy, a word he obviously did not understand, but he shouted on top of his voice, "Your daughter will be hanging from a meat-hook, like the other traitors."

By now mother was on her knees and I could not bear her humiliation any longer, as he went on raving, that she had born such a creature as I . . . only an earthquake swallowing me up, would have prevented me now from retaliation . . . and when he finally picked up the wall telephone to call the police, I reached for my Luger, which I had thankfully early in the morning pushed under the sideboard, after the POWs had left, and pointed it at him. I shouted at him, "The only traitor in this room is YOU, plus you are a coward for good measure; hate me, but my mother is your wife and you are prepared to hand her over to the Gestapo."

Cold sweat stood on his forehead as I moved closer with my gun, but my mother screamed, "Please don't kill him, for God's sake," and to my amazement, she walked over, removed the receiver from his hand and replaced it. Somehow, he just stood there like frozen to the ground watching my movements, and when I turned my back, cursed and threatened to get even with me, but my own battle was over, a confrontation of wits and wills between good and evil, or so I believed. My admiration belonged to my mother, who under stress proved her maiden name proud as KERN meant seed . . . one puts it into the earth to grow . . . and she stood 6ft. tall, and faced possible death at the hands of her husband, to protect me.

Now more than before, I depended on Major Schoepf's military influence and power to see us through this latest crisis, which could lead to total destruction via my vengeful stepfather, who one could never trust. I therefore agreed to travel with the major to Linz, where his HQ was, and hurriedly packed my few belongings; two pullovers, one pyjama and of course my Luger and extra bullets, in case we were ambushed on route. What strange philosophy to adapt, I thought, being educated in a convent . . . or should I have been trained on a guerilla camp? Had I really lost all feminity, yet men desired me fervently? I asked myself. But until the final victory, as promised by Prime Minister Churchill was ours, I was pledged to fight and make the supreme sacrifice, if called upon. It seemed everything was out of control now, yet I had to continue with my mission and accept this wild romantic love of the last man I was about to escape with.

As expected, Major Schoepf came with a staff car loaded with food, medical goods and arms, and off we set for Bruck and Frohnleiten, where his powerful Nazi friends owned a villa. We got a great reception, with enough bottles of wine and toasts, to last me for a lifetime and to my astonishment, none for their genial Fuehrer? "WHY" I asked.

"We are not going to be killed for Hitler in the last days of war."

How loyal indeed, 360,000 young men froze or were killed at Stalingrad; most of them are fellow Austrians. How noble could the Nazis get, once defeat stared them in the face?

The Kolb's villa was luxuriously furnished and they gave us the guest-suite, which pleased Hans no end in particular; it was the first time we had shared rooms alone, and his idea of breeding this "Master race" was constant on his mind; now was his chance, or so he believed!

It was such a pity that Major Schoepf, who was a handsome man of thirty-eight years of age, a brilliant solicitor in civil life, could not divorce himself from this Nazi ideology, resurface and embrace a new future. He still believed in winning this war, however silly it sounded to me. We stood on the balcony overlooking the beautiful scenery, whilst a few yards away the defeated transports of the German Army rolled past, grinding to a halt; and on many trees, young soldiers who could not face the slaughter any longer, were hanging with posters around their necks — "I am a coward . . . or deserter". In stark contrast, there was I, again protected by my enemies, if only for a few hours, clad in furs placed around my shoulders by my hostess Frau Hilda Kolb and admired by my lover 'the Major'. What a crazy existence with the RAF planes flying overhead dropping bombs on the transports and shattering the windows. As the night approached, I became apprehensive of how Hans would react, my biggest fear having sexual intercourse and possible pregnancy; thus I had to stall him with the only weapon at a woman's disposal. 'Those days are here once more', and he believed me! Five days reprieve, I thought, hoping of another miracle.

Frau Kolb and I interchanged the cooking routine, and as it was my job this day, I fried some chicken pieces, when suddenly full air alarm was given and without any hesitation, I picked up the frying-pan and began running down the street, but no-one found it odd. Only the fast approaching Mosquito, which dived down at me, and I could see the pilot smiling, and the force of wind blew away my food. Just a tiny piece I saved; picking it off the ground, and with the empty pan, I waved at the disappearing plane shouting, "Damn you RAF, I am on your side you fool!"

When I reached the shelter, I put down my pan and a tiny little hand reached for the dirty small piece left and stuck it under his shirt. He seemed on his own, this little boy, and cried, so I hugged him and we both cried together, each for a different reason. I asked him his name, which was Peter, and he told me his papa was killed in Russia, and that he only had a granny, who was very very old now. "God have mercy," I said to him, but he did not understand and I only wished that I could have taken him back to the villa and given him a good wash, and plenty to eat, at the expense of those greedy Nazis, who caused all this misery in the first place. I wrenched myself away from this little boy and dared not look back, or I should have taken him with me, regardless of the consequences.

Upon my return from the shelter, I sensed danger seeing a grey car standing by the front door, and the to me, well-known Gestapo getting out; one spying around the villa looking for footprints. Are they searching for me, I wondered?

I saw Major Schoepf at the window waving me to walk away towards the road, and I obeyed. I soon noticed that he followed me to have a talk.

"We have to leave at once, or we shall be trapped between the partisans (how wonderful I thought) or the fast advancing Russians. Perish the idea," the major added.

Yet I could not resist a little jibe at him, asking gleefully, "Where are your Tiger tanks now, Hans?"

"Bogged down in the snow," was his fierce reply, and I had to pretend not to laugh out loud.

I told him providence had come our way, for me it was a certainty and just in time, with only two days of stalling left, and I insisted that we had to split up and make our own way; he to Linz, and I to my aunt's place in Graz, as I could not possibly "endanger" him in his military car, with orders, only to carry fighting soldiers. I paused for a while and thought to myself, the sort of fighting I would do was certainly not in his Nazi book of rules and regulations, as ordered by his now supreme commander, Adolf Hitler.

How controversial could one get? Perish the thought, you little girl and thank heaven for small mercies, getting as far as Frohnleiten, with only 25 km to my target, Graz. I only wondered, how many more obstacles could there possibly be?

After the Gestapo departed, Hans and I told the Kolbs of our separate plan to leave, and they agreed that it was for the best.

Hilda packed my rucksack with plenty of food and my clothing, but I decided to keep my Luger close to my body in a holster, just in case?

Hans and I said our last goodbye in the lounge. He held me so close that I could hardly breathe; but what did it matter, I owed him that much, for he protected my mother and I for the past five months during his command in St. Stefan, and now it was all over. The misguided Nazi officer on the run, who for some reason had fallen in love with me, like a man possessed; and as I looked into his grey-blue rather sad eyes, he said, "I never made a fool of myself over a woman, but you aroused a passion in me I never knew existed. You just had to walk past me with your sexual arrogance, and I was falling to pieces."

Of course, I promised to write to him, only where, was a puzzle, and if it ever reached him, the war hopefully would be over. Also he assured me that he would be coming back looking for me, wherever I was, of which I was certain; but for me, a new chapter, the final struggle to reach freedom was beginning and Major Schoepf, just another man of the past.

It was approx. 3 p.m., and heavy snow began to fall again. But there was no other solution, an easy way out, but to soldier on en route to Graz via the nearby forest, full of hidden dangers. The rucksack on my back felt a ton weight, with snowflakes blurring my view and a hundred thoughts racing through my mind, some recalling the days of sheer bliss . . . or did I imagine it all? I smiled to myself. What saved me so far from certain death? . . men . . . silly men . . . they did so much, for so little. I pulled my woollen cap over my ears and buttoned my grey weatherproof blazer over my Luger, still reviewing my past. Those men, how many had there been; their conflicting loyalties, spent passions, ups and downs.

The gruelling journey continued; soon it got really dark, yet the sky above me was deep-blue and beautiful and I wondered if up there lay the secrets of our fate, as the wood engulfed me more and more. How much longer will I have to be on the run, the vengeful revolutionary? But then if one's close family is to be annihilated by the Nazi thugs, you want revenge, and the only way I could do it was by taking up arms and fight. Rather strange, men fell over themselves to get hold of me . . . I had began to hate them, for their cruelties they committed in the name of Hitler, and justified by saying, "We only obeyed orders" . . . shooting in cold blood old women, pregnant women and children fleeing from their burning homes! What sort of warfare is that? They never scored with me, gasping and panting the chase was on, but I always managed to put up a defence of some kind to protect my honour. Was I indeed a trail-blazer for all women, who wanted to be free, from bullies, or being herded together in labour camps, prepared to be breeding machines under a dictatorship? Stop thinking you little fool, get a move on . . . and put more miles between you and the enemies, perhaps surrounding the perifery of this wood? By now, I was counting my footsteps, making every effort to keep going, when I spotted a little wooden hut and made for it, when I heard voices coming from the inside. My heart missed a beat; how foolish of me to think it would be empty with all the deserters on the run, and I listened intently, to what I could possibly hear went on in this 8 x 10 ft. shed?

Thank God, one sounded cultured, as he outlined their awful shortage of food, asking the others to conserve their strength by saving the pills he had kept in reserve for his dying patients. Obviously he was a doctor, I thought, and renewed hope charged my brain, and I was prepared to offer some of my food to bargain to let me stay, until daylight? I simply had to rest and take this chance, or freeze outside in the deep snow . . . all my deliberations ended at knocking at the door, which I did rather firmly. Was it to show that I was not afraid, or sheer bravado?

The door was pushed open from the inside, which was in

darkness, and I could only see the outlines of three men with guns at the ready, asking me who I was?

"On the run, like you chaps," I said cheekily, holding my hand on my own Luger just in case, although I would not have stood a chance in hell against this menacing trio, when one shouted, "It's a girl, come in and warm yourself."

Carefully, I walked in. As they turned on their oil-lamp and shone it in my face, I noticed two were sailors and one obviously an army doctor, with the rank of captain, and he introduced himself as "Dr Held," adding, "but my name is badly misplaced." Held in German meaning hero . . . thus, ridiculing the latter meaning.

Gallantly, he put his fur lined coat on the floor for me to sit on, and I thanked him, looking into his fine-cut face, with deep-set eyes. We smiled at one another, why, there was nothing funny about us being here in this mess, but circumstances like these, showed perhaps the mettle, we all were made of.

I offered them some of my food, which was in my rucksack, and eagerly they began to open it, taking out a whole chicken, bread and apples. "All this and heaven too, for us?" Dr Held asked, and I nodded, and within seconds they started to eat like crocodiles; including the small bones vanished, and I realised, that hunger was the most humiliating state to be in, and the primitive urge to fill one's stomach came first. Sitting down in the corner, I watched them with half-closed tired eyes, always a little afraid what they may do next. Yet I had enough guts left to believe . . . the fed-animals usually go to sleep? Indeed, I was right. They lay out their blankets and dozed off, with the exception of Dr Held who sat next to me and told me why he deserted from Stalingrad and Russia, being fed-up cutting off frozen limbs, often without any anaesthetic. "I can still hear those screams of the men," he added, pushing his coat over my legs to get warm.

I flinched, but he told me not to worry, no-one will rape me, pulling my cap over my ears.

Suddenly, the sailor was sitting up, suggesting they played cards, to pass the time, and the other followed suit, with the doctor fetching some cards from a bag, which was behind my back, excusing himself for disturbing my nap.

At the same moment, Franz, the U-boat survivor bent over me and exclaimed, "Let's have a good look at you, little girl."

But Dr Held told him to behave; but I was wide awake, pulled up my legs and held my Luger under my jacket, which seemed noticeable.

Now all hell broke loose, and the other named Otto began to be aggitated, and he screamed at me, "You silly bitch, we are not going to rape you, we haven't got the strength for a start, so put your gun away, or I shall have to take it off you.''

Dr Held jumped to his feet, telling Otto to pipe down and think of their escape-route, for tomorrow. Now all three started to row, as I sat there frightened to death, just praying the doctor will talk some sense into them. The air was thick with recriminations, as to WHY they had lost the war, with Dr Held accusing the sailors of letting British seamen drown like rats, once their ships had sunk.

"We had our orders from Admiral Doenitz," Franz countered.

All I heard were orders, it made me sick and I also intervened, stating what I thought of Hitler and his gang. Suddenly, I was not afraid any more, we were all in one boat, on the run and possibly confronting death by hanging, IF caught by the still, on the look-out, SS storm-troops. When I finally made myself heard, they stared at me as if I had two heads, and agreed with my version, that the big Nazis were still alive, whilst millions of others had died on behalf of them, and for what? I stood at the utmost corner of this shed, and proudly displayed my Luger and I told them that anyone coming closer, would be dead, and that I had fought in the Resistance since 1941. Franz grinned, but when he noticed my finger on the trigger, he moved backwards and saluted in a daft fashion.

Is that how the would-be conquerers, behaved? I wondered. And I could not help but pity them.

Dr Held placed his coat over my shivering shoulders and told me to sit down and have a little rest, or sleep if possible, as he could see how tired I was, and I obeyed, nearly falling into his arms fatigued.

Otto pushed also his coat like a cushion for me to be comfortable and I thanked him very much, glancing at his gaunt face.

How strong was my willpower? I thought, to stay enough awake, to know what was going on around me. Oh please God don't forsake me now; and as I was about to doze off, I heard Otto say, "What a lovely face she has, Doctor," and when he agreed, he added, "I'll bet she could steam up your specs, and raise your blood pressure."

However, Dr Held told them to be quiet and let me go to sleep, still holding his arm under my head and by now, I looked upon him as my protector and friend!

Was I dreaming, or having a nightmare, because I could hear shots fired and loud voices?

"Come on out, or we will burn you out, like hornets, you scum.''

I was on my feet and Dr Held gave the orders for Franz to investigate. It was still dark and snowing, with a strong wind driving the snowflakes into the hut. I lay on the floor as Franz crept outside, returning the fire, shouting to us "They are SS-lers, down the ridge below us, I can only spot two," and he added "and we are three, and a half!!"

The latter was me of course, and I smiled in the face of death and thought, 'Why do men think they are so superior?'

I gathered my few belongings together, laying on my stomach, and Dr Held motioned me to creep outside; my Luger at the ready and only to fire, when necessary?

"That's a tall order for only one half of their group," I whispered and Held smiled at me as if he felt sorry for me touching my arm, when fierce shooting started from all sides. I saw a tall SS soldier in front of me. He threw a grenade towards us which exploded. I felt a sharp pain in my knee and screamed, yet, I don't know where I got the strength from, I managed to fire my gun at the other man and he fell into the deep snow, throwing a second grenade. By now blood was gushing from my left knee and Dr Held rushed over to examine the wound, and I shall never forget the look on his face, which said don't panic, or we are all lost.

Otto came from behind to see, what happened and the doctor told him to fetch his bag, and within seconds he jabbed an antitetanus injection into my thigh, took out my pyjama trousers from my rucksack and bandaged the knee, as firmly as possible.

The shooting had ceased and Franz came along anxious that we must move out from here, before other SS soldiers spotted us — indeed two of them were dead and one ran away, so we had a little breathing space!

Dr Held kneeled beside me, keeping me warm with his lovely coat, and although I pretended to be calm, inwardly I was on fire, terrified to be left here to die, by bleeding to death. The doctor made a major decision, putting his head on the chopping block, by insisting that they carried me to the nearest hospital; thus of course, possibly risking being arrested and charged with desertion. What a dilemma, and I realised I was at the mercy of three strangers on the run, and as they looked down at me laying there in the snow, partly covered by Held's coat, they seemed so much taller, angry looking, or was I losing control of my faculties, I wondered?

Otto said, to leave me in the hut.

"NO NO," I begged in despair, with tears choking my words, "just drop me outside the hospital and run away." I suggested "Someone will take care of me, please for God's sake, don't leave me here alone to die."

I was frantic by now and Dr Held comforted me, the best he could, and told the others, if need be, he will carry me alone. I weighed about eight stone fully dressed, but to carry me in this deep snow was impossible, yet he lifted me and tried, with the bandages soaked in blood, he swayed and had to sit down, holding me on his lap.

Franz exclaimed, "Damn it Otto, have you lost all self-respect, the girl gave us her food and fought with us, like a soldier. Let's give the doctor a hand."

My condition had so deteriorated, that I hardly understood what they were saying, yet they wrapped me into a blanket and began to carry me along. Slipping into unconsciousness, was like leaving all turmoil behind — with heavenly peace at the other end; and when I awoke, I was in hospital with Dr Held holding my hand saying, "It's all over now, the operation was a great success and soon you will be dancing again on two legs," adding, "perhaps even with me." I kissed his hand, which he pulled away, bending over me, to whisper that he had managed to hide my Luger at the bottom of my rucksack, now in my locker next to me.

Did I really deserve all this protection from a stranger, I had only met a few hours ago? Or is there a certain destiny between all of us? Or deep down a dynamic person dwells and rises to the surface, sweeping away all current fears and problems?

Hans Held's hungry face was close to mine and he told me that I had nearly reached the breaking point, like him, when he decided to desert from his unit. He brushed back the curls from my forehead and said emotionally, "What strange fate has put you in my path girl? You came with the snowstorm and suddenly made my heart tick faster."

"It's simply compassion on your part Dr Held," I insisted.

But his lips came closer, and his soft brown eyes flickered, and he answered with conviction in his deep voice, "There is something magical about you Burgi, you are half-child, and all woman at the same time, trying to save humanity, whilst I obeyed orders, watching thousands die, on the battlefield."

The air raid sirens sounded once more and a nurse came in to ask me if I wanted to be taken to their shelter, but I said "No" and Dr Held retorted, "Great, I always wanted a woman with a positive mind, yet feminine and smouldering, who sets me on fire, when I least expect it."

Two voices were vying for my attention, caution and confusion, with my saviour so very attractive and close. I realised that war has no respect for people, and demands sacrifices, and every moment could be precious and every word, the last one utters. Hans Held and I were simply thrown together in a snowstorm, to become strange companions on the run. Yet I was afraid for him to say this fatal sentence, "I love you," reality was against us?

The suddenness of our circumstances had overpowered us both, and we were just one man and one woman, bewildered and in need of tenderness, after the horrific atrocities our young eyes had witnessed . . . and so be it. We could hear the heavy bombers flying above us, but for us the world stood still. No fear, no pain; forgotten the possibility that Held may be caught and be shot for desertion. "Now I have a real reason to stay alive," he said, with me thinking of the worst, 'How dare I?'

I changed the subject and asked him if he liked music, and who was his favourite composer. "Need I ask . . . Strauss and Lehar," Hans said, when a Dr Binder, who introduced himself came in, checking if I was alright, or needed some tablets to ease the pain.

"What pain?" I asked.

He then pointed out what great help Dr Held was assisting with the operation, and he only wished to have more doctors like him at the hospital.

"I know, he's wonderful Dr Binder," I replied, holding both hands of the man who saved my life.

The all-clear sounded and Dr Binder departed with a wicked little smile, as IF he guessed our secret.

"Can we trust him Hans?" I asked anxiously, emploring Dr Held to leave at once.

But he just sat down on my bed caressing me, assuring me of his love and trying to make me laugh by telling me, "My brother is also a doctor; he specialises with ear and throat troubles, and I am the lung and heart expert. Thus I have started with yours," adding, "and convinced you of my integrity, *gnädige Frau*?"

"Herr Doctor," I said, "please convince me some more."

And Hans did by holding my head and kissing me long and gently; but it was heavenly and I recalled my favourite song, *"werd' ich bei seinen Kuessen erbeben . . . werd' ich das Wunder der Liebe erleben . . . einer wird kommen, dem werd' ich gehoehren,"* and Dr Held's kisses gave me the answer; will I tremble, when he kisses me . . . shall I know, that the magic of love, has come at last . . . he will have come . . . to whom I belong."

Indeed, at this moment of my life, Dr Held fulfilled all those dreams, and very soon after we said *"Auf Wiedersehen,"* but not goodbye at his request, and of course he gave me his address in Graz and we promised to contact each other, as soon as it was safe to do so.

Never before had I owed so much to a man, as this one . . . my LIFE, for all it was worth to me and the people who loved me.

The hospital, although nearly deserted by its staff, functioned the best it could, and an elderly nurse was looking after me and I was convinced that by now every one needed a friend to vouch for, with the Allies on the doorstep. My biggest fear was being discovered with victory in sight; thus I made every mental and physical effort to get well, and Dr Binder was truly astounded at my quick recovery and the healing of the wound; attributing it to his skill as a surgeon of course, and my youth.

Whatever the case, within ten days I was discharged in the first week of April and given a letter referring me to the Orthopaedic Department in Leoben, for futher treatment.

The sirens were howling as I left thanking Dr Binder and his staff for all their help. He asked me where I was heading for, my reply was to meet up with my "fiance" Dr Held in Graz, and no further questions were asked, for which I was thankful. Indeed, the situation was too funny for words, but more like a "Thriller" and "Merry-go-round" at the same time; yet the very thought of getting caught, made me shiver with fear.

My discharge from the hospital was very ordinary, as if the war had already been over and my belief, that everyone now needed a friend to start anew was evident, yet the danger of a last minute hitch was always possible. I could hardly put my feet to the ground and test my strength, but my new-found spirit and the very thought of Dr Held willing me to be safe, so that we shall meet again, worked wonders. "Love is all powerful," I said to myself — "and laughter, the best medicine, and the most pressing problem now, to get back home to my mother's place."

Unforseen circumstances altered my plans and I kept thinking of Hans Held, with a sudden sense of elation entering my life. Was the price of his silence, too high? His name alone plunged me into a passion that matched my own, and the realisation came with such clarity, that it simply stunned me. How could a stranger hold such sway over my emotions, in which love and desire were one? Of course, he had seen my naked body when they took off my clothes and prepared me for the operation, but then as a doctor he had seen many women undressed. I began walking towards the main Brucker road and checked my rucksack. Thank God my Luger was, as Dr Held said wrapped-up in my pullover and loaded. How did he manage to do this I marvelled, when a woman from across the crowded street shouted my name.

It was Paula, I knew her from St. Stefan and she was the sister-in-law of the woman looking after my mother, and I told her briefly that I was fresh out of hospital and why I was there in the first place. Military transports were rolling past us covering us with dirty snow, yet Paula insisted that my pretty face will get us a lift. "Some hope," I said "we had better plan out our 25 km walk and when to rest." Women with small children were fleeing past us, with all sorts of goods and overloaded prams; the sights were unbelievably ugly; dirty rags covering their heads. And so we marched in columns, the snow driving against our faces. Survival of the fittest was the order of the day and I teased Paula that no-one so far had noticed my good looks, also my knee began to hurt badly and we decided to rest by the roadside like two tramps, and I took off my cap and let my hair blow in the wind.

"That's the answer to our prayer; your lovely hair" she shouted. "Men always notice women's hair."

"You're a witch, Paula" I replied laughingly, when low and behold a car halted, asking us where we were heading for?

"St. Stefan."

"So are we," was the answer, and the driver took my rucksack and pulled us into the loaded vehicle, only to be greeted by a German captain decorated with the Ritterkreuz and Brillianten.

This was sheer madness as far as I was concerned, or a comedy of errors; a 'Hero of the Thousand Year Reich,' giving me my last lift home?

"My name is Klaus, what's yours Fräulein?" he asked with petulance in his voice.

"Burgi, Herr Hauptmann," I said forcing a smile to my lips, at being so lucky, getting a ride.

"What a strange name," he scowled teasingly. "I shall call you Tiger, after my tanks. His eyes covering my entire body.

But frankly I did not care, as long as I did not have to walk this dreadful crowded road, not to mention the awful bad weather.

Klaus introduced his driver to us. "Fritz," he said stiffly.

Paula turned towards me as he insisted that she sat next to him, gripping her arm; and soon we felt the coiled tension between us. But what choice had we now, to escape?

The captain lit a cigarette and drew the smoke deeply into his lungs, watching me with half-closed eyes and began to boast about his victorious battles in the Balkans and how the Fuehrer personally presented him with the Ritterkreuz in Berlin in 1943 — plus the splendid reception afterwards.

Klaus was still inspired by his glorious Nazi-past and kept raving and ranting about it to me, promising to turn the tide of war in their favour soon, when the Fuehrer's "Miracle-weapon" will be used — a bomb so powerful, it would destroy all of London.

I just sat there next to him raining fire and brimstone at the enemies — which of course unbeknown to Klaus included me, and I dared not to think of my fate should he ever find out before I reached my home?

The bumpy ride continued and Fritz began to curse the many unfortunate people in his path and he shouted at them! "Hang on tight," Klaus said and "Lay your face against my shoulder." And when I did not oblige, he pressed his chest against my breast, but I shoved him off me.

"What's wrong with you girl? I want the pleasure of feeling your curves." His hands moulding my hips, and his eyes gleaming with sardonic amusement, and his teeth flashed a terrible smile.

Paula got very worried realising what was going on in the back, but she was unable to intervene, or even say something. How could I immobilise his hands, I thought, as by now he was bringing his body closer in anger and frustration and he mentally stripped away my clothing. I cried out as if in pain, and he laughed, "What's the matter? Don't tell me, you've decided to be coy, my pet. You would look great in a red dress, my enchantress" he blurted.

"Why?" I asked curiously, trying to understand the mind of this Nazi officer.

"It reminds me of the blood that was spilled killing my enemies," adding, "in point of fact, Hitler ought to give me more medals for services rendered," he said laughingly.

What a cruel statement and if I ever needed proof, that the likes of Klaus were madmen, he gave me that answer.

I drew breath and asked him what he was going to do with me once we had reached St. Michael, and his reply was devastatingly frank. "I can do whatever I please," and suddenly I felt naked, although I was fully dressed and his voice was as sharp as the blade of a knife.

I stared at him in disbelief as he lifted my chin, "No, no" I cried, as his eyes travelled over me, slowly moving across my breasts, then skimming down my trouser-clad legs, and a chill went through my blood, "no, please no," I whispered.

But Klaus was beyond caring and shouted at me "Yes, it won't be that bad, if you obey my orders," bringing my body closer to his.

As though hit by a rocket, the car halted and Klaus demanded to know, why?

"It's all this rabble on the road, Sir," his driver exclaimed!!

Thank God, for that, I thought, giving me a breathing space from this depraved madman.

He got out to remove some of the "obstacles" with his whip, hitting an old woman over her back, telling her to "Damn well get out of my way!"

She looked at me, sitting there in the car with a hateful glance, and I could not blame her, thinking that I was one of those "tarts" following the troops around. God have mercy!! So that is what the Nazis called the fleeing population . . . rabble . . . women, still breast-feeding their babies, wrapped in rags, holding their hands out for a crust of bread, ignored and abused by this heartless officer. How ironical, I who had fought them every inch of the war, should be sitting next to one, and I who would have shot them a hundred times in combat, given a chance.

St. Michael came in sight, and with it the Gasthof Eberhart, where during the war, and my working days at the HQ in St. Michael, I often had my lunch; such as it was . . . soup and bread, if I was lucky!

By now, I despised this man, I told myself frantically, as I scrambled out of the car, with Klaus holding me by the waist, when Frau Eberhart, a fierce Nazi and the wife of the ex-Commander of Kiew came to greet us. It was obvious, they both talked the same language and victory was still possible; yet the latter's husband by now was a POW in Russia's Siberian camp, and had little chance, to boast about his glorious days as a Panzer major, rounding up the civilians to be shot, as Frau Eberhart had told me a few months ago.

She viewed me up and down, and said to Klaus, "Where the hell did you pick up her, she was always in trouble with her superiors at the HQ, in St. Michael?"

"On the road," was his reply. Klaus run his gloved fingers through my curly hair and exclaimed, "Properly washed, this girl could be a knock-out Frau Eberhart, don't you think so?"

"Well," she groaned, "I could do with some loving myself for a start, so why bother with her?"

At this moment, I wished that he could see in her the Mona Lisa, or the Queen of Sheba, just to take his mind off me — but after walking around me in fun, he insisted, that I was the number one in his harem, and that was that!

His driver Fritz had joined us and Klaus offered him Paula, but he declared that he loved his fat little wife more, as Paula was too skinny for sex.

Frau Eberhart led the way into the Gasthaus and there already were many drunken soldiers, mostly deserters, shouting their odds, to the amazement of my 'Hero'. Klaus was furious and at once took command by getting onto the table, and fired a shot in the air, thus making himself heard, with his driver holding on to Paula and I by the arm. "The turning point for our final victory, is NOW my comrades," Klaus shouted. "Our Panzers will hold the enemy and destroy them! General Kesselring and General Guderian are consolidating their positions, and driving the British and Yanks back into the sea.''

"What sea — our milk pond near here?'' one soldier shouted, and in response Klaus fired a shot right through the mouth of the daring corporal and his blood was splashing all over the place, setting of a near panic amongst the other men, yet, no-one challenged Klaus. "Any more defeatists to follow suit?'' the enraged and out of control captain screamed; and at that point I pondered over my own fate, should this lunatic tackle me.

Paula, who was frantic by what she had witnessed, clamped herself on me, with Fritz pointing his pistol at us both, telling us to be sensible and keep close to him . . . or else . . . the latter sounded awful, having been through sheer hell in the last two weeks, only to be confronted by a sex starved Nazi Klaus.

Paula was shrinking back, intimidated by the action of Fritz. But no man ever got away, so far, with intimidating me with a gun, so to his horror, I produced my Luger and in the turmoil of howling soldiers I told Paula to leave via the back door — which she did. Our bodies were only inches apart and I moved past Fritz like a cat going for the kill. His fingers tightened on the trigger. Was he going to kill me? My pulse began to race, there was a message in his eyes, and he shook his head.

"No,'' he said clearly, "I simply could not shoot a girl without thinking of my own wife at home . . . I only wish . . . '' he had not finished the sentence, when Klaus came over blazing mad and grasped me by my blouse, dragging me forwards, his hands moving along my neck, slipping into my hair, his eyes riveted to mine, and then his mouth touched mine — one last stand!! one desperate attempt to cool him down, or blow me into oblivion.

"To possess my body Klaus, you will have to kill me, I am afraid,'' I added.

"You are not worth it Tiger,'' he said breathlessly. "Film stars have been fighting over me — so who are you to turn me down?''

Time and reality slipped away and I thanked God to save me from this monster, whose calculating vanity was stronger, than his sex drive.

"Can I leave now please?'' I asked, as they dragged the nearly dead soldier by his legs, and threw him outside into the snowy road; and the dirt splashed my already filthy clothing. Surely, I could not possibly have any feminine appeal to any male? Even to these depraved soldiers of the Third Reich?

"Not so fast mein Fräulein, I have not finished with you yet,'' Klaus said, with a glass of schnapps in his hand; and I reminded him that I was not good enough for him, trying to humour his ego, but it misfired.

"What did Othello say to Desdemona, after he strangled her?" And Klaus got hold of me once more by my neck. "A kiss . . . one more kiss . . . that's what this black fellow said — and I want this kiss now, do you understand mein Fräulein?"

I wiped my lips in disgust, and he got hold of me and flung me into the road next to the dying soldier and shouted, "You ungrateful bitch, I gave you a lift, and that is how you repay me," and he lashed out into thin air, turning in a ring, drunk.

What a spectacle indeed, the Herr Ritterkreuztraeger, the equivalent of the proud VC, dancing like a bear in the snow, firing shots in the air to frighten me and some others, who cowed down, begging him to stop.

I heard in the distance a motor car, which was very familiar to my ears; that of Franz Winkler, my partisan boss, and he came fully prepared with several other men, all armed and I knew, this would be a fight to the finish, one way or the other?

"Get in this car at once," Winkler shouted to me and I rose, my Luger still in my hand and proceeded to do so, when Klaus barred my way — 'that's it,' my brain telegraphed — but from the back of the crowd stepped the village doctor, and with him was the local police chief and they said coolly to the captain, "You are under arrest for killing this soldier," and they got hold of his arms and bent them backwards, and he winced a little as they marched him away.

I could not believe my eyes, with Frau Eberhart, the only one protesting at this 'outrage', as she called it; but soon was silenced by the rest of the onlookers. Franz Winkler brushed me down, and said with his famous wicked little grin, "Our recklessness, is only matched by your bravery Burgi," and he whirled me towards him.

"Why did you risk your life for me now?" The blunt question darkened his eyes.

"Because you needed rescuing from the savages, and you've done enough to obliterate the Nazis, and we are proud of you."

We drove off in the old car with two rifles still ready at the back windows, leaving behind the chaos of human beings, fighting in the street, littered with military debris and would-be conquerors!

Exhausted, I leaned back into the arms of Franz Winkler and looked up at him, tears streaming down my dirty face.

"We've won my girl, it's our victory as well, Burgi, the only thing that matters now," holding a knife he said; and he ran his thumb along the worn handle. A wry smile touched his lips and he hurled the knife far out into the by-passing river, and he explained, "Dammit, there's no point in keeping it now that they are dealing with this SS pig Klaus."

I looked into his eyes and could see the blazing anger, as he was always out to revenge the treacheries against his family and friends, and he had faced danger willingly. Silence stretched between us as we drove on homewards bound, when all of a sudden, I said, "You know Franz, he called me 'Tiger', after one of his tanks."

"Say that again," Winkler demanded, and I did, and he roared with laughter!!!

At last, there was still a sense of humour left in him, and the other three men. I thought with victory at our fingertips for the first time in months, I felt a tiny flame of hope flicker in my breast, and I laughed through my tears.

The General

The 8th of May 1945.

Sporadic shooting could still be heard in the nearby mountains, and we all longed for the final curtain of war to fall. It was a time when one never knew whether a knock on the door spelt danger via the retreating SS soldiers, or the advancing Liberators.

We; that was my wounded mother aged sixty, who was being looked after by an elderly woman called Frau Seiner, my stepfather of the same vintage, and myself at the ripe old age of twenty-two, had found refuge in a deserted 'Alpenhaus', up in the mountains near a place called Lobning.

I, an 'old' member of the Resistance, actually caught myself thinking about what I would do with my share in the victory of the Allies. Where this imagined reward would come from, I truly had not considered. However, as my posessions after the seven-year Nazi reign amounted to practically nothing, because everything we owned had either been taken or confiscated, I naturally assumed that some kind of compensation would find its way to us.

All I had to show for seven years of fighting was what I was standing in. This consisted of a grey dirty riding outfit, which was complimented by a blue sweater that had shrunk from excessive washing, so much so that it appeared to be glued to my body.

My mother, who was a rather plain but kind and fairly religious sort of woman, prayed daily for some kind of normality to return to our lives, happy in the knowledge that she too had done her bit in altering the face of history.

My stepfather was a rather handsome man, but he was the odd one out, because he was always complaining how hard done by he was, when he really did not know the meaning of the word. He had been a stablekeeper in charge of the 'Wehrmacht's' horses and as

34

such had not incurred quite the same hardships as some people, I knew. He was like a weather-vane, turning in whichever direction the wind of politics was blowing.

It was my mother, who gained all my respect and love for her courage and bravery, whereas for his attitude alone my stepfather came under my category for contemptible. There was truly not a lot of love lost between us. To him I was the 'rebel with a cause', born of a woman who in his eyes was a courageous fool.

The Germans were steadily retreating and the Allies advancing, but to us there appeared to be no real sign that war was now finally over, except for one thing. The silence outside seemed almost unreal, at times even frightening.

Now and then I looked out of the small windows of the 'Alpenhaus' just to check that all was really as it appeared. Occasionally, I would wander about looking at our ammunition and rifles in case of ambush. 'Restless' is probably an understatement of how I felt.

It was just such a day, when Frau Seiner suddenly shouted: "Oh God, there are hundreds of soldiers coming up the hill." A quick glance confirmed my worst thoughts. They looked just like an advancing horde of ants.

I reached for my Luger and bolted the door. "The SS will never get me alive," I said to my stepfather, who had already mounted his rifle on the window seat and motioned us to get down.

The voices came closer and got louder and were obviously Russian. A sigh of relief in our midst was closely followed by a bang on the door with a firm order to open up at once. Josef, who had been our Polish prisoner of war, and who spoke fluent Russian and German, stood in the door flanked by two tall Russian officers. He quickly interpreted that I was to meet a general. He pointed down the road where three black cars were standing like a funeral procession.

A little unsure, but smiling, I agreed, looking around me, wondering why there were so many heavily armed men being sent to escort one little girl to their leader.

A stocky officer got out of the first car. His clear steel-blue eyes looked right through me. His face had strong features but his mouth indicated a ruthless streak of character. My first impression was that he would be a formidable adversary. His medals almost outshone the sun as he saluted me, with Josef introducing us: "The victorious general welcomes you, because you served in the Resistance and contributed to victory . . . . . ".

Josef bowed low as if he was in fear of the Russian, but I told him to tell the general that I was very flattered that he sent so many men to collect me . . . . . . as the Gestapo, only sent two . . . .

The stern face of the general gave way to a big grin, and his foxy eyes surveyed me from head to toe; I could see that he fully understood my little joke.

At this point another officer approached and whispered something into his ear and I was told through Josef, that we were off to a victory party.

"Like this?" I asked pointing at my scruffy appearance.

The general just uttered three words, "Krasiva . . . . mnoga krasiva . . . " and motioned me to get into his car.

Josef later explained that this meant beautiful, and thus the first words in Russian were almost a repeat of 'Fate' and history for me. And I thought to myself if it were really possible that after all the fighting of the last few years to stay alive, I would have to do it all again, only this time to fight off, the advancing victors!

I was sandwiched between the general and his aid in the back of the car. Josef sat by the driver. The general and his aid were firing questions at one another, none of which I understood. I knew then and there that I would have to learn Russian, because their voices droned through my head like machine-gun fire.

At last our little convoy arrived at the villa 'Edelweiss' which had been known to me in my Resistance days, because it had been occupied by a rather unsavoury SS colonel and his mistresses. It had been known as the local Bordello.

We got out of the car, onto a hurriedly rolled out red carpet, and were soon surrounded by guards presenting arms. We were greeted by a few high ranking officers and ushered towards the entrance-hall, where to judge by the noise, a rowdy party was already in full swing. I was terribly embarrassed when I saw the rooms filled with immaculately dressed officers, all in their dress-uniforms, and there was me, in my threadbare trousers, not to mention the state my riding boots were in, whilst the man on my arm, the general, looked as if he had stepped out of a shop-window.

The general must have sensed my uneasiness, because to my utter amazement he suddenly pulled my arm closer to his and said in perfect German, very quietly: "They will only notice your face and figure Fräulein."

This statement took me so by surprise, that all that I could think of was to thank the general for his compliment, and to remark how excellently he spoke German. He smiled and we proceeded to make our way, through rooms filled mainly with officers.

As we mingled with the crowds, my eyes suddenly focused on a big, tall man who stood out as he was dressed in civilian clothes, and dwarfed most everyone around him. He had his back to me and I could not help but wonder what type of face was attached to this impressive stature.

Servants arrived with large silver trays, on which stood the finest crystal glasses filled with drinks. The general handed me a glass proposing a toast . . . . 'to the great Stalin', to which nearby officers followed suit. As did I. But when drinking what I believed to be wine, I nearly collapsed, for it was neat vodka and hot as fire. The general laughed, slapped me on the back, making me splutter and cough. It was not until someone brought me a glass of water, that I managed to regain my composure, only to be drowned in the most humble apologies of the general.

As the evening passed, my mind returned to the tall civilian and my eyes began to search the room. Just as I pin-pointed his tall physique, he turned and obliged me with a full view of his face. And what a face it was; handsome, strong and full of expression, with burning eyes which had obviously guessed my curiosity, as I suddenly became aware, that they were returning my intent gaze. I pulled myself up as if waking from a day-dream, but it was already too late. The tall stranger was making his way towards us. The general who had been engaged in conversation with his aid, seemed pleased to see this man, and immediately turned and introduced him as Captain Karl Steiner.

This tall, handsome man, then engaged me in conversation, referring cynically, to being a 'guest' at the Mauthausen Concentration Camp, where he learned to speak Russian, by befriending a Soviet POW.

Now face to face with Steiner, I was even more convinced, that he could be the perfect man for me, as his arresting eyes sank into mine. Here I go again, I thought in a panic. I began telling him about myself. How I had fought in the Resistance and outlived the nine lives of a cat.

He smiled, showing his tiger-like teeth and replied: "Well, with your looks, Himmler himself would have helped you escape . . . . "

There I was placing Steiner on a pedestal, whilst he was pushing me down. How dare he? I exploded, telling him, that I expected more respect from a fellow partisan.

The general obviously understood the gist of our conversation and made sure that the incident did not blow up into a full-scale row, by ushering me over to the food table, urging me to make the most of the opulent amounts laid out before us.

It was true, I had not seen food or tasted anything like it, since before the war, as my anger melted with the delicacies before me.

Before long, the general reminded me that he would have to leave soon and asked if there was anything else that he could possibly do for me. My mind returned home to my ill mother, and I asked Josef to explain to the general about my mother's illness and that she needed to move back to our flat, and that most of all she needed medical attention.

The general listened most carefully and immediately ordered his aid to get a doctor; a woman, by the name of Olga Petrovich; his driver, and of all people, Herr Steiner, to take me home and attend to all my wishes. Before I could say 'Thank you', he saluted and left.

Steiner smiled, gave me his arm and I accepted, because Josef stayed behind and I needed an interpreter for the Russian woman doctor.

Steiner had organised the car and arranged for me to sit next to the driver, whilst he got into the back with the doctor.

'She is most attractive,' I thought, as I seated myself, catching Steiner's rather wicked smile, as if he had read my mind.

However, my own concerns soon turned towards home, where my mother lay ill, and all other thoughts vanished, with the possibility of getting her better via this doctor.

The events of the last few hours had thrilled and bewildered me, as real-life adventure, was once more entering new dimensions.

With hardly a word spoken during the entire journey home, we arrived at the Alpenhaus at past midnight to the great relief of my mother, who had by now began to worry.

The doctor examined her partly-healed fleshwounds and diagnosed that my mother suffered from undernourishment and physical exhaustion. She gave her an injection, and left tablets which would soon make her better. Captain Steiner also explained that he would send an ambulance to take her down the hill back to her flat and that he would arrange that someone would come in daily to take care of her, until she was well again.

I was delighted and thanked them both for their help. They left around 2 a.m., and Steiner teasingly reminded me that none of this would have been possible if the general had not been 'bedazzled' by me.

The very next day, as promised, an ambulance arrived with two men, who carried my mother down the hill and moved her gently back into her flat in St. Stefan.

I went with her, but to our amazement found the flat tidy and heated by our neighbour.

When we enquired how she came to be there, she replied that she had been given orders by the all-powerful general, and then proceeded to tell us how she had been evicted from her own place, because her husband had been a member of the Nazi party.

Although I detested the Nazis, I could not understand the need for these actions, and made up my mind to speak on her behalf to the general, when next I saw him.

Indeed I did not have to wait long, as during the afternoon, the motorcade of the general arrived. The driver got out first carrying two large suitcases, which he took right past me into my rooms. He was followed by the general, who promptly dismissed him and the two officers who were following him. However as they left, they stuck what seemed to me to be a poster to our front door. Josef, later explained that this was an order, protecting our home from being searched by Russian soldiers.

When finally we were alone, inside my room, the general told me to open up the suitcases. I did so with trembling hands in astonishment at the sight before me! I thanked him very much, as such clothes and furs, I had only seen in films. The general, delighted with my reaction, began picking up some of the furs, shouting: "These are yours to keep, I order you to try them on at once."

This was sheer madness, but wonderful, especially as the threadbare clothing I was wearing was all I possessed. Thus, I picked up a heavenly silver-fox cape and flung it over my shoulders, loosening my hair, by combing it through with my fingers.

The general sat down and watched me closely. Even though his eyes were mere slits, I could see them glint happily. "Krasiva" he would repeat over and over again, and when I asked him to explain, he just said "Beautiful, very beautiful". He added another word "malinka" meaning child which made me think that he was humouring me and I said so, stating most strongly that I was no longer a child, but a woman.

He took no notice, stroked my hair and kept calling me "malinka"! He then showed me a photograph of a beautiful woman with a young girl on her lap saying: "My wife and child. The Germans murdered them, and I loved both so very much."

One did not need to speak Russian or any other language, in order to understand the anguish, for tears were running down his face. My life felt insignificant compared to the sacrifices this man had made. Somehow the clothes before me became obsolete, and I put them back into the case. The general, however, insisted that I kept them, and demanded that I dressed myself up for this evening's 'Gala-Performance' at the Leoben Town Cinema — where he fully intended taking me. I had really little choice, and before he left, he spoke to my mother, in very broken German, assuring her of every attention from his staff.

"Such a kind man," exclaimed my mother, and with that, any reservations I had dissappeared, as I went to get ready for the evening. I simply had no time to try on all the lovely items in the suitcases, but I picked a crimson velvet dress, with tiny silver buttons on its sleeve, wearing it with a white fox fur, which covered me twice over. Preparing my mother for a shock, our neighbour made an announcement of my entrance to my mother's room. She sat up, only to fall back in disbelief, at the sight of me before her.

At 7-30 p.m., the general arrived in full dress-uniform, and gasped when he saw me.

The drive to Leoben lasted half an hour, and upon our arrival we were greeted by the manager of the cinema, bowing very low, as if we were royalty. It was all so like a fairy-tale. There I had been only yesterday, a poor, hungry Resistance fighter, and here I was today, on the arm of one of the most powerful men in the Steiermark, dressed like a queen with people standing to attention. This was definitely too good to be true, but whilst it lasted, I made up my mind to make the best of it.

The film-show was good and afterwards local dignitaries presented the general with flowers, which he duly placed into my arms. Also masses of letters were handed to him, and I guessed what they contained, petitions from Nazi victims.

When the general had a few moments to spare, he glanced at the pieces of paper; but most were written in German, and he handed them to me. Some were pleas to return goods like furniture, animals and cars that had been confiscated, and I tried to interpret, as best I could.

"You must learn Russian" said the general, to which I agreed, asking him to lend me his dictionary.

I searched for the necessary phrasing to explain the pieces of paper, but soon the general became impatient saying: "Tonight, you are my guest, not my interpreter."

From the cinema we drove to a villa, which he said belonged to his aid. As we drove into the forecourt we could hear dance music and laughter. Captain Voroshevsky greeted us and made us welcome. Everything came to a halt as the general entered, and it strangely brought to mind the Communist slogan, that all people are equal, making me think 'That obviously some are more equal than others'.

However, I was just about to enter a new era of splendid living, thus I adapted myself to the events at hand, and as if he was guessing my thoughts — Steiner came over and asked me to dance.

I agreed, more so, because I wanted to prove to myself, that this stupid infatuation with a stranger, was all that it was . . . . . a stupid infatuation. He swept me into his arms and with half-closed eyes looked down at me saying: "The general is watching us like a hawk . . . . and I for one, would not like to cross swords with him."

"How thoroughly decent of you Karl" I snapped. "We must remember to say goodbye, before we get to know one another."

The music was playing and creating enchantment. As we danced I thought about the reasons that we two must be put in separate compartments, a place for everything and everything in its place . . . . especially me. I was still lingering in Karl's arms as the last notes of the band resounded: '*Jeder Druck der Hande . . . . deutlich mir's beschrieb . . . . er sagt klar, s' ist wahr, es ist wahr, Du hast mich Lieb.*' 'Yet, every pressure of your hands . . . . clearly describes to me . . . . it's true, it's true . . . . you are in love with me.'

With a deep sigh, he released me, thanked me for the privilege of dancing with me, and handed me back to the anxious looking general.

In decisive response, Sacha asked me to dance with him, as if to endorse his rights over me, asking me to sing the words to the waltz.

I obliged, singing: "*Wie ein Wunder kam die Liebe uber Nacht, heut hat mir das Gluck beim Waltzer zugelacht . . .*" "Like a miracle, love came into my life . . . and Lady Luck smiled at me during the Waltz . . .".

That was the gist of the translation and it seemed as if the general understood much more German, than he let on.

When the dance was over, the three of us had drinks and caviar with delicious Russian salad. The evening progressed, and we drank and were merry. Then out of the blue, the general made an announcement that I would entertain them with song and dance.

A little bewildered I asked him how he knew that I could, to which he replied: "I have read your file at the Gestapo HQ from A to Z."

So without further ado, I went over to the band and told them which music to play. I took off my bolero, moved across the stage and began: "*Stern von Rio, Du könntest mein Schicksal sein. Wie leuchted Dein Zauberschein nur mir allein . . . .*", turning before the general and his party.

He took hold of my arm and kissed it in fun, but a tingling went through my whole body. I kept my composure, finishing the song to rapturous applause. Our host then declared the party over, thanking me for my lovely singing.

The dancing and singing had made me thirsty, and I begged for a glass of milk, to cool me down. With a suppressed smile, a servant fetched me what I wanted, but when I had finished my milk, I discovered that the lounge was suddenly empty, except for the general and I.

Nervously I looked around as the general began fingering the tiny straps on my gown. "Call me Sacha, it's short for Alexander," he said.

I cautiously disentangled his fingers from my straps and reminded him that he was a great general and that I was only a little village girl.

He paused, looked at me intently and said: "I am only a man falling in love, making a fool of myself."

I got up and moved backwards towards the wall, with the general in close proximity. Pearls of perspiration stood on the general's forehead as his grasp became passionate.

"Please don't" I pleaded. Sheer terror visible on my face.

The general was startled and loosened his grip. Whether he had actually realised that I was still a virgin, I don't know, but his manner became very gentle and soothing as he said: "You are both, a malinka, a child, and also a woman, a very beautiful woman. You must understand that I am not only a general, but also a man. However, I will not make love to you, unless you come to me of your own free will."

My expression visibly relaxed and almost gave way to a faint smile.

"That's better," he replied and kissed me.

It was then that I realised that there was no difference between a Western man and his Eastern counterpart. The world around us can alter, but the physical demands are the same.

Before he drove me home, he poured us both a glass of wine and proposed a toast to our friendship, and newly-founded understanding. From that moment on, my relationship with the general had taken on a serious note, and I was cautious of not upsetting him too much, as I needed his help, in caring for my mother who was receiving medical treatment, under his direction. Also, I thought, that maybe through my connection with him, I might be able to help some of the other people I knew who had lost everything; even the roof over their heads; i.e. like our neighbour. Only time would tell.

Back home, my mother was surprised at the news of this newly-founded friendship between the general and I, and advised me to be careful. Suddenly, an incredible life lay before me!

The next morning, I was just putting my new wardrobe in order, when there was a knock on the door. It was the local doctor, Dr Ehrlich, who had come on foot, because the Russians had confiscated his car. Through people in the village, he had heard that the Russian general called on us, and thus he had come with his urgent request of help, from me.

"I will do everything I can," I promised the doctor, who had been a firm anti-Nazi and who had lost one leg during the First World War, making the use of a car a necessity, as walking with one wooden leg was really not a comfortable way to make his rounds as a doctor.

Whilst we were still in conversation, other people arrived, all wanting help with something. One thing was sure, news of my 'importance' now travelled so fast, and the villagers had lost no time in trying to make the best of it by demanding my help.

The arrival of the general's car added further chaos, and only when I agreed to take all the bits of paper with complaints written on them, was I able to shut my door, and get dressed. The general awaited me at 11 a.m. at his headquarters in St. Michael.

With mixed feelings, I departed like an envoy on an impossible mission, yet, sure that I had at least to try, to convince the general that it was wrong, to just take everything without due regard, for anyone.

The general's villa was guarded like a fortress. There were soldiers everywhere, and the car was stopped at several control points; all manned with menacing-looking guards . . . . . machine-guns at the ready; before we actually reached the house. My driver had to explain several times who I was, before we were allowed to proceed.

When I finally reached the big front doors to the villa, I was led into an ante-room and told to wait, closely watched by a further two guards. I began to feel quite uneasy, when at last the general appeared in the door, to rescue me from his own men. Indeed this had been rather an unnerving start to our newly-founded friendship.

The general took me into a large room, where to my amusement, I found a nicely framed photograph of myself on his desk, just like the one that had gone missing from our home shortly after the Russians' occupation. I mentioned this fact to the general in the little Russian I could muster, but he just smiled, reminded me again to call him Sacha, took me in his arms and kissed me.

However, I was in no mood for romance, and soon freed myself to move to the other side of his impressive desk. I took a deep breath, pulled myself up to my full height, and then almost attacked the general verbally, with the matter foremost on my mind! Namely, Dr Ehrlich and his lack of transport, placing the car number and make, which I had written down on an envelope firmly on his desk, saying: "You must get his car back at once."

The expression on the general's face changed, he clenched his fists and banged them down hard on the table, shouting at me: "I am the general here, not you, and if I were to shoot every German under my jurisdiction, it would be nothing compared to what they did to the Russian people. How dare you to command me to sort out what they have brought upon themselves?"

"Two wrongs don't make one right," I countered.

But he did not understand my meaning, and started raving at me: "I shall have you put in prison, if you go on saying that my soldiers are thieves!"

Memories of all that I had experienced under the Nazis welled up inside me, and made me shake with anger. I was not about to capitulate now, thus leaving the general in no doubt, as to my version of justice. Almost screaming at him I said: "Here . . . lock me up . . . . put the handcuffs on me . . . . just like the Gestapo did in 1943." I held out my hands.

The general's face lit up with passion, as he pulled my outstreched arms towards him, and before I could say anything else, kissed me into silence. Tears were streaming down my face, and I was wondering, whatever made me think, that I could stir up so much trouble and hope to get away with it?

Moments later, he sat me on a nearby couch and told me to calm myself. He got up, picked up the telephone and engaged himself in, what appeared to be a heated argument. I could just make out the name of Dr Ehrlich, when his face became taught and his voice, sharp and commanding. After a short pause, he nodded an affirmative, and giving out another order, and put down the receiver.

He sighed . . . . . looked over to me and said: "They've traced the car and will take it to the doctor's residence . . . . satisfied????"

I was so happy, I just jumped up, rushed over to him and gave him a big hug. He kissed me and said: "I really will have to get on with some work now Burgi, I'll get the driver to take you home, and then I'll see you this evening."

When I got back, my mother informed me that I had a visitor, one of my oldest and dearest friends from the Resistance days, a girl called Martina. She also lived in St. Stefan, not very far away from me, but due to the whirlwind of events, after the initial arrival of the first Russians in our village, we had not spent very much time together, as the Liberators, had made the Resistance obsolete.

She told me of the latest batch of Russians that had arrived in St. Stefan. Apparently, whilst searching the local pub, they had found barrels of wine, hitherto undiscovered in the cellar, and were drinking themselves into a stupor. Martina was worried that they would start searching the houses, taking everything, that took their fancy.

She urged me to come and sleep with her in the attic of the barn, where we used to hide in the old days, from the Gestapo.

I, however maintained that the general's notice on our front door was all the security I needed and that none of his soldiers would dare to cross our threshold uninvited, adding, that she would probably be safer with me! She would hear none of it and made her excuses and left.

It was now late afternoon and I decided to get ready for this evening. I was about to change my dress, when two drunken Russians burst into my room. They just grabbed me, and under screams of protest began manhandling me, in turn.

My mother, who had been in the kitchen preparing tea, came running into my room and seeing what went on, she managed to grab one man off me and shouted for help at the top of her voice.

As I only had one to contend with, I managed to struggle free, and jump out of my bedroom window. I promptly fell down a ten metre embankment, which was covered in stinging nettles, and landed at the foot of the stables belonging to Martina's house. I dashed to the outside lavatory and locked myself in.

Unbeknown to me, the general had arrived just in time to help my mother to her feet. She was almost hysterical as she pointed to the two fleeing soldiers, running down the stable yard. The general shouted "Stoi", and then fired two shots, one of which found its target, and killed one soldier outright.

On hearing the two shots, I ran out of the toilet back up to the house, frightened that my mother had been shot by those two drunkards.

Out of breath, on the doorstep, I was confronted by the general, revolver still in his hand, saying: "I have executed him."

I stood there, trembling, with hundreds of blisters all over me . . . . . . my clothes torn . . . . . . tears of relief streaming down my face.

Sacha tried to put his arms around me to comfort me, but I pushed him off me in anger, shouting: "This is what your soldiers do everywhere, when they are drunk — your orders obviously, mean nothing to them."

Sacha ushered me into the house and sat me down on the sofa next to my mother. He then declared that there was only one solution, and that was for me to stay with him at the villa, which he had commandeered as his own living quarters. I looked at my mother, and he immediately told me not to worry, as he would organise for Frau Seiner and another woman to come and stay, so that I could leave in the confident knowledge, that my mother would be cared for.

My mother also urged me that this was for the best, saying "They are not interested in us old women, but there is really no better protection for someone as young and pretty as you — Go on, I will sleep better at night, knowing that you are in safe hands."

As this had now been agreed upon, I was moved by Sacha, that very evening into his villa, in St. Michael. He very politely showed me where I could clean myself up and left, kissing my hand and he said: "From now on, I shall take care of you, my Malinka."

The guest suite was furnished luxuriously, with a beautiful brass bed, an antique velvet settee and the floors were bedecked with exquisite Persian carpets. The bedroom also, had a large French door leading to a balcony, which at a quick glance, appeared to be encircling half the villa.

But all I wanted was the bathroom, and there I stayed in the bath, for what seemed like hours, scrubbing and scrubbing until my skin was raw. Although there was nothing left to clean off, I felt unclean and could still feel the mauling hands of those soldiers all over me. The anger and frustration of being once more just a pawn, hurt even more than the stings all over my body.

I stepped out of the bath tub and stood in front of the full length mirror, as if seeing my naked body for the first time. It made me shudder to think, that even though my body was covered in blisters and scratches, I felt totally bewildered! Was it still not enough to deter the men in his world? There was Sacha, offering protection . . . . but only, so that he could have me for himself. This and many other thoughts were racing through my mind.

I began to shiver, and decided that I had better pull myself together; so I went into the bedroom and searched through my suitcases, until I found my silk pyjamas and matching dressing-gown. I quickly put them on and was just about to get into bed, when I heard footsteps coming down the corridor, followed by a knock on the door. Before I could say "Come in", Sacha was already standing half-way in my room.

When he saw the scared expression on my face, he said: "It's only me," took me by the arm and led me through the French doors onto the balcony. We gently walked the full length, until we reached another set of French doors, which were open, leading to a bedroom of equal splendour, to the one we had left behind. He ushered me in, sat me on a leather chair next to his bed, saying: "Burgi, you — will have to come to this room of your own accord, and then, I will make love to you! I don't want to be your conqueror, it has to be sweet surrender on your part," and he kissed me.

When he finally released me from his tender embrace I replied: "All I want for now, is a good night's sleep and peace; Good-night Sacha." I promptly withdrew to my own rooms.

Yet I had a sleepless night tossing and turning, wondering if Sacha would keep his word, and whether I would weaken under his pressure. My resolve was strengthened by only one thought . . . . . . the burning desire . . . . . . to be loved by this man, called Karl Steiner. Yet, I tormented myself with thoughts, of the Russian woman doctor called Olga and Steiner making love.

It was not until the sun was blazing across my pillow, that I finally awoke around 11 a.m., the next day. There was an exquisite air of silence and splendour about the place, which made me curious to explore my new home. When I had dressed and was just about ready to set off on my adventure, a soft knock on the door made me jump! This was followed by a more audible knock, by which time I had grabbed the nearest vase, run behind the door and shouted "Enter".

A kindly-looking face appeared, which broke into a broad smile, when it pin-pointed me behind the door ready to pounce with the vase. I realised that I must have looked somewhat ridiculous, and immediately put the vase down on the floor.

The woman came in and introduced herself as Frau Koeller, the caretaker of my new home. She quickly assured me that I would be quite safe in the villa, as the general before leaving, had issued her husband with an automatic rifle and orders to shoot any intruder.

'What a situation to be in' . . . . I thought, ... 'being protected by a Russian general against his own troops.' But I was thankful and said so, and accompanied Frau Koeller to the kitchen, where a hot pot of coffee was already waiting.

Over breakfast, she told me that the villa had formerly belonged to a high-ranking Nazi official who had fled into the American zone near Salzburg. She then gave me a guided tour of the place, through many luxurious rooms in one of which I discovered, a grand piano. Happy at this find in my golden cage, which was what

I now perceived it to be, I sat down at the piano and gave Frau Koeller a sample rendition of my favourite song. She was delighted.

As the days went by Frau Koeller became my servant, cook and friend. She and her husband were also very loyal to the general, doing everything he asked of them. Even large dinner parties at a drop of a hat were never too much for them, and soon, Sacha's parties became a nightly event.

The general demanded of me to be his hostess, to be seen in eloborate outfits, and to sing and dance for him, and his guests. Love-making, as far as Sacha was concerned, was still strictly taboo, and I admired his resolve to stand by his word, as befitted an officer and a gentleman. He only indicated his physical desires for me when we were alone, but thankfully this was a rarity, as he was much in demand with officers, calling on him almost every hour, and his other duties keeping him busy the rest of the time.

It was now the end of May and my favourite flower the lilac was in full bloom, and at our fabulous dinner parties, the rooms were always filled with the heavenly-scented blooms.

I soon adapted to my new role as good hostess at these functions. Usually between eight and twelve officers attended our soirees, but to my surprise, were never accompanied by any ladies. Only once did I meet two attractive Russian women, but these were officers, also and rather oddly, they did not openly resent me. However, Sacha was not very polite about them, calling them big and man-women! In comparison, he was probably right, I was only 5ft. 2in. tall, with measurements of 36, 24, 36 — whilst these women, although attractive, were 6ft. tall and heavily built. What amused Sacha most, were their size 8-boots, whilst my tiny size 4½ — looked like children's shoes, next to them.

To Sacha, I was just his beautiful Malinka, and he showered me with worldly goods — which he had taken from my former enemies, the Nazis. How paradoxical life can be I thought, there was my Communist commander, shunning his own women, but giving me every luxury possible, yet referring to capitalists as parasites.

I had truly come to like Sacha, but it was mostly a gratefulness, for all he had done for my mother and I, yet I still did not have it in me, to be humble.

The general often teased me, saying that I was his 'Waterloo' and quoted 'That all was fair in love and war'. But I swiftly reminded him that now was peace-time. He would hold me close and reply: "Only when you let me make love to you, will we enjoy peace-time,

my *darughia"*. He would then refill his glass with vodka, drink it
down in one, smash it extra hard against the wall, as if to squash
the passion inside of him.

I often asked myself, how I was hoping to keep him at a distance,
when at the same time, I was tempting him with sultry songs and
dances, tantalising his senses and then wriggling out of his reach?
The answer of course was this strange quivering ache for Steiner,
inside of me, which took on the form of crippling confusion
between mind and body. It was somehow ironic that Steiner was
keeping me at a distance, while Sacha did his best to draw me into
his web of emotions, in, which I wanted no part. And so began just
another hectic day, with interviews, followed by tears and even
bribery, as I was getting ready for another of the general's parties.

Six weeks had gone by, and it became obvious that the Russian
troops were here to stay, if not in our village, certainly in Austria,
for several years to come. The question was only, for how many?

My Russian had improved tremendously and could be described
as fluent. I had made such progress that I was able to translate vital
incidents accurately, and Sacha lost no time in giving me the post,
as an interpreter at his headquarters. He had done this more as an
official bluff, to have a genuine reason for keeping me close to him,
then for the grievances of the people, he now ruled. But day by day,
I managed to influence him to relax the inhumane laws of the Stalin
era, just that little bit more.

Soon the news spread that I was a 'Dolmetch' for the general,
and streams of people who had incurred losses by the Russians,
descended on the HQ with the oddest requests. My prestige grew by
the hour and some even called me 'Frau General', much to the
amusement of my mother, whom I visited regularly, and who by
now had regained most of her health. She also by this time, had
become genuinely fond of Sacha who in turn adored her Austrian
dialect, even though he could hardly understand it.

It became a strange relationship between us three, as my liaison
work began to take up more and more of our time.

Even at the villa, I was besieged by the most unlikely assortment
of people, from professional opera-singers, to the cobbler in the
street; everyone telling me their grievances in great detail; their
losses of goods, from grand pianos to plain everyday work
benches.

One such person told me about an incident that would have made
me laugh, had he not been so seriously upset when he related the
following to me: "The Russians just came and loaded it all up, and
for good measure they asked me what time it was, I looked at my

D

watch to oblige . . . . and off they took that as well.''

Perhaps the funniest of all complaints came from an elderly retired army officer, who had his false teeth stolen. I did not know how to tell Sacha, without both of us losing credibility, before his staff. As all cases were dealt with in terms of urgency, I went straight over to Sacha's office to get something done. As anticipated, he laughed so much when I took 'this most urgent' case to him, that the whole place appeared to be coming down around our ears. Finally, however, he did sign the relevant documents, stamping them, and putting his official seal on them saying: "After this crazy business that you have got me involved in, it will be a small miracle, if I am not executed by the KGB, when they find out, how I am conducting the affairs of state in the Steiermark, chasing after false teeth." But on a more serious note he added: "Oh *darughia* . . . . my darling . . . . what is there left, that I will not do for you???"

He was right . . . . there was not much that he would not do for me, but every day there were more petitions caused through problems that had been created by the general's troops in the first place. And so I had no misgivings whatsoever in exploiting the general's help. However with each day that passed, it became more and more of an uphill struggle to deal with all the problems.

Whilst discussing these matters with my mother one evening, she remarked on her astonishment at the turn of events, since Austria had been liberated. She explained that she had fully expected life to return back to normal after the war, as had we all; but instead we were no better off with restrictions everywhere and life had become more chaotic than ever. In fact our homelife had been completely turned upside down by the Russian victors. Not only by my involvement with Sacha, but also by my stepfather's appointment as head stablekeeper of the 'Wehrmacht's' horses, which of course now were the property of the Russian Army. This had meant his staying on at the alpenhaus in the mountains in order to look after the horses, which had to be left out to graze as there was no fodder in the stables. And it seemed to me that my mother was missing him. To me this had been a godsend as my stepfather and I never really got on and I was glad to have my mother to myself.

My work at the headquarters of the Russians, began more and more to resemble a doctor's surgery. SOS calls arrived by the hour and even Sacha said "Will it ever end?" I was tempted to tell him that with 55,000 Russians occupying as small a country as Austria, it was no wonder that it was impossible to exercise any real control. His soldiers were living by the motto: 'to the victor the spoils' and with no supply lines of their own, it was hardly surprising that they just plundered wherever they went like a hoard of locusts. However, I knew that there was little point in renewing this argument with Sacha, as to be fair, he did his best to help wherever possible. In fact if he could not find what had been confiscated, he usually found a way to replace it.

One such incident concerned a young woman with a child, who had her goat stolen. The goat had been the provider of milk for the baby, and when she found one morning that it had gone from the gatepost, where she had tied it the previous night, she was totally beside herself, frightened that the baby would die. In a very distressed state, she beseiged me for help. When Sacha got to hear of this, he soon realised the impossibility of finding the goat alive and unbeknown to me found a replacement which he simply ordered to be tied to the gatepost without any fuss. When the young woman returned to me a few hours later, I dreaded having to tell her that I had not managed to trace her goat.

However, to my amazement she replied that it did not matter any more, and thanked me for the lovely cow, that she had found tied in its place.

I immediately went and thanked Sacha, who smilingly replied: "Well we couldn't let a baby starve!" Adding further, "Exchange is no robbery."

Later that same day, my Aunt Berta phoned from Leoben, where we had been to the cinema. She owned the cinema, and she cried as she told me that her cinema organ and red carpet had vanished in the night. For the latter, I could see a reason, but what could anyone want with such a big heavy instrument? So I begged Sacha to help her.

There was only one problem . . . . . . the Russian word for organ. A translation for this word was to be found nowhere. So I sat down in a chair in Sacha's office, mimicking the playing of this instrument. I must have appeared to Sacha like a puppet without strings, my arms and legs going everywhere. I reduced Sacha to tears of laughter. This was made worse, when his aid walked in, with two prisoners of war, reporting for work duty, looking with dead seriousness at my impression of a marionette, obviously wondering . . . if it was THIS, which turned the general on?

To save his reputation, Sacha pulled himself together in an instant, and sent us all on our way, making a quick exit himself towards his private chambers, to release his obviously suppressed laughter.

On this occasion we were lucky, I finally found someone who gave me the Russian word, after I decided to make a sketch of it and the organ was recovered.

My aunt was delighted, and as thanks, she promptly offered to give the general and his staff, a private showing of any film of their choice.

Sacha left me to decide what films we should see, and a few days later we all went to view the famous Zara Leander film called 'Heimat'. This film had some lovely Wolga songs in it, thus pleasing the Russian officers of Sacha's staff enormously, resulting in my being complimented, at my choice, by everyone.

From that day on Sacha came to rely on my judgement in various matters more and more, and often told me how proud he was, to have me at his side.

Another month went by, and the Russian Occupation was now accepted as part of our daily lives. Only the Nazis still in hiding, trembled with fear of discovery, as the very thought of being sent to Siberia, brought them down on their knees to pray, to escape such a fate.

The people in my village looked upon me as their MP now, and their requests for help became less sporadic and more organised, thus leaving me a little more time, for my own pursuits. So besides my work at the Russian HQ, I also now had time to go back to my singing lessons at Leoben, with an old wartime friend, an ex-opera singer, Frau Lucy Koerting. She had opened up her acting and singing school again, in the Hauptplatz at Leoben.

Lucy and I went back a long way, and had been through some dangerous times together. I was the only one who knew that she was partly Jewish and had managed to shield her from persecution by her own mother-in-law. Now that it was all over, I once again was able to bring her food, only this time as payment for my lessons, which she happily accepted as being far better than payment in cash, as even with money, food could only be had at a price on the black market.

As I had to account to Sacha for my time away from headquarters, he usually sent his driver to take me and collect me. Upon return from my lessons, he was always pleased to listen to my progress report, as he knew how important this was for me.

My ultimate aim was to turn professional. Lucy was a tough teacher and pointed out every fault, but also praised my talent and I appreciated that her efforts to turn me into a first-class singer and actress were actually producing results.

In her opinion, I had the voice and looks . . . . and in that order . . . . and a career on the stage was a foregone conclusion. This encouraged me to work very hard, and under her guidance I studied operatic roles like 'The Countess Maritza' and songs from the

Lehar operettas 'Der Csarewitsch', which became my own favourite.

Following one such rendition of what I had learned that day, Sacha suddenly announced that he would give a special musical evening at the villa a week to the day. Of course when I heard that Karl Steiner was among the guests to receive invitations . . . . . yes invitations, everything was always done formerly amongst the Russian officers, I began to rehearse like mad just to get my act perfect. I wanted so much to make an impression on this man.

I decided to wear my own pale green brocade evening dress, which had a halter neckline with a very low décolleté. It was decorated with a large silk rose of the deepest red and emphasised what I considered to be my best assets.

At last the evening was here, and the general took my arm to accompany him while greeting the guests, most of whom I already knew.

However, the man I was waiting for, made a late entrance, together with the woman doctor, Olga. She was in her best white uniform, which fitted her like a glove, and I wished that I had more to offer, than my alabaster white skin and my thirty-six inch bust.

Sacha played Master of Ceremonies, and made the announcements of my songs, to the rapturous applause of his fellow officers. A hired professional pianist accompanied me, and played the introduction: '*Einer wird kommen . . . der wird mich begehren . . . einer wird kommen . . . dem werd ich gehoeren.*' '*Werd Ich bei seinen Küssen erbeben? werd Ich der Liebe Wunder erleben?*' The translation of which reads: 'One man will come . . . . who will desire me . . . . one man will come to whom I'll belong.' 'Will I tremble when he kisses me . . . . will I experience a love of ecstacy?'

I sang this song with full conviction for Steiner alone, but he hardly glanced at my direction, being far too preoccupied, kissing Olga's hand! This upset me no end, and I decided that I would just have to find a way, for him to notice me. Was I just plain crazy, or was I just trying to relive a lost passion with a partisan friend? This friend had been killed, but Steiner did so remind me, of my long lost flame. 'Oh God, let sanity prevail' I thought, as I looked over to the two love-birds in the corner of the room — and continued with my second song and dance.

I danced past the officers, who cheered me on with drinks in their hands, as I sang: '*Stern von Rio . . . . du könntest mein Schicksal sein . . . . nur du allein.*' 'Star of Rio . . . you could be my destiny . . only you alone' . . . and I smiled at Steiner, who now blatantly stared at my low neckline, with obvious delight. He murmured something that I did not understand and I sang on, my ego considerably lifted. '*Du kennst die Leiden . . . und auch die Freuden . . . du kennst das Geheimniss der evigen Liebe. Wie schön hab Ich mir erdacht für heute Nacht . . . . . .*'. 'You know the tears and also the joys . . . you know the secret of eternal love. How I have imagined the joys of the forth coming night . . .'. I ended up in front of Sacha who was just spellbound by my performance.

Finally, when I stopped singing, he got up and shouted 'Bravo, bravo, you were wonderful my darling' amid the applause of the rest of the room. I could hardly hear anything with so much noise, when I heard Josef whispering into my ear: "You've really done it now, the general will grant you anything after this performance."

If I could have had anything, I think Steiner's head on a silver plate would probably have been the prize, for the way he had taunted me this evening.

The party was over and the guests were departing and also Karl came over to say goodbye. He kissed my hand, but only because it was expected of him. I am sure that he realised the chaos of feelings he managed to arouse in me, when ever he was present. But he seemed to enjoy teasing me. And so it was on this occasion, when he could hardly wait to say, as he left: "Burgi, you exceeded your talents tonight, but I am sure . . . . . the general will reward you."

If I had been a cat, he would have felt the sharper end of my claws, but as it was, I demurely thanked him and bid him a good-night.

When everyone had finally left, Sacha was still drunk with the spell my songs had weaved, as we ascended the stairs with him kissing my bare shoulders, wishing me a good-night.

The next morning I got up early, to join Sacha for breakfast, as I saw this as the ideal opportunity to bring up a matter that had been on my mind for some days now. I had just wanted to catch him in the right mood! And after last night's success it had occurred to me before going to sleep, that Sacha would no doubt be in a good mood this morning and would hopefully not wish to deny me a little concession. This matter concerned a young man, called Rudi Pfanner, who was the cobbler's son. He had been forced to join the SS during the last weeks of fighting and was now at the Russian prison in St. Michael, awaiting a sentence of death, or Siberia. Pleading for the boy's life and freedom, I explained to Sacha that he had no choice but to join. It was either that, or be shot by the Gestapo.

Sacha jumped to his feet shouting: "How dare you try to weedle such concessions out of me, by taking advantage of the fact that I love you. For God's sake woman, I have my honour as a Russian officer to consider . . . . this is not a case of a lost goat! I am dealing with an SS prisoner, not some helpless child.''

"But he never fired a shot" I screamed at the general.

But Sacha refused to listen to me and stormed out.

Frau Koeller had heard most of the rumpus and warned me to look after my own affairs and leave the general to take care of his. After all, they had, in her opinion, not made the general, military commander for nothing.

But her reasoning did nothing to convince me that the general was right, to send this seventeen-year-old boy to Siberia or to his death.

The general avoided my company for the rest of that day and I began to wonder whether that then was the end of our affair.

The next day however, Sacha gave me an even sterner lecture about who was in charge at HQ, and that all SS men deserved to be shot a hundred times over.

My strong sense of justice was aroused and I couldn't stop myself from saying that maybe 90% were criminals but what of the 10% that were ordinary fighting men just doing as they were told?

Sacha got hold of me by my shoulders, shaking me, and shouting "I am an officer in charge of thousands of men who have seen their comrades die by the hands of these SS men . . . . . and you want me to release one of them? Are you crazy?''

Now we both started shouting at one another, with Sacha threatening to send me to Siberia. I promptly challenged him to do so, as there was obviously no justice anywhere, stating that I could see little difference between the Germans and him if he persisted in blindly handing out punishment.

He slapped me across the face and instantly regretted his action, taking me into his arms to undo what he had done. The tension had been too much, and in order to make up, he told me to write down the young man's name.

Later in the day, he made enquiries, and found out that the boy's father was on a Gestapo wanted list in connection with the escape of two British POWs. The very same men who also I had helped on their way after discovering them in our stables all those years earlier.

Now that the whole truth came to light, Sacha was also made aware of my involvement in their escape and probably out of compassion changed his mind about Rudi Pfanner.

When I left the Russian HQ that day, I knew that the boy would be released. I also knew that Sacha might even have to face charges, upon his return to Russia for bending his rigid rule book. I was really more aware that for as long as he was here, I knew, that nothing would get in his way in his attempt to woo me, not even his Soviet bosses, not while they were thousands of miles away.

Since Sacha had taken command of my life, I was forced to live in two worlds; that of mine and that of his, which had no reality value for me. And I often wondered whether one day I would wake up and find that it had all been just a dream.

It was now June, and I was contemplating a brief visit to my wartime friend Martina in order to focus on some reality again. As this meant travelling to St. Stefan, I of course needed travel papers with the general's approval on it. None of this would have been necessary if I had allowed the driver to take me, but I wanted to spend the day leisurely with Martina, without the continual reminder of time in the form of the driver hanging over me. When I explained all this to Sacha, he agreed to let me go my own way as he knew Martina and admired her for her bravery against the Nazis. As St. Stefan was only 5 km away, I left with Sacha's best wishes for a happy outing.

My friend and I shared a special closeness and decided to use these few precious hours together to visit her brother, who was living at Knittelfeld, only some 4 km away, to take him some food parcels.

Martina was frightened to go anywhere on her own and was glad that I agreed to go with her. There was only one problem, to get into Knittelfeld one had to pass over a tiny bridge which had a Russian guard, like a border post on it, and no-one was allowed to pass without the relevant documentation. This seemed to me utterly ridiculous and I assured Martina that I would have no difficulties getting across. So we arranged for her to accompany me to the bridge and that I would return as soon as I had delivered the parcel.

Martina and I parted at the bridge and I proceeded alone. There appeared to be no-one around so I continued with hurried steps, until I heard a Russian soldier shout: "*Stoi*" 'STOP' and I did. As I turned, I was confronted by a soldier with a rifle, who then subsequently arrested me. He pushed me along in front of him until we reached his little hut at the start of the bridge, where he asked me in Russian for my 'pass'. I pretended not to understand him and began shouting in Austrian at him, expressing my disgust at not being able to walk in my own country freely over a silly little bridge.

He grinned at me and telephoned his captain for help . . . . . he certainly needed it . . . . . with me now ready to go on the 'war-path'. A young officer arrived, took charge and marched me to the local jail, where I was locked up in a cell which already contained five other women.

As the door shut behind me, I realised that all my demonstrations were of no use. The women there pointed out to me that their crime for being there was exactly the same as mine, as they also had crossed the bridge without a pass, and that really I should save my breath as they had been complaining for weeks.

Having been cocooned at the general's villa in St. Michael, I had forgotten what the other Austrians still had to put up with. It had needed an incident like this to make me aware, of the shocking conditions that still existed. Indeed, some of the women looked absolutely terrible, with just a minimum of food and little or no sanitary attention. One young woman, stood out in particular as she was menstruating heavily and had no means of cleaning herself up with only male guards on duty. No wonder she was too ashamed to ask them.

When my mind had absorbed the awful sight before me, my temper at these savage conditions got the better of me and I started banging on the heavy iron door, until my hands were hurting.

"Give it up dear, and relax. They don't care if we rot in here," said one of the women.

I was going to tell them who I was, but feared their ridicule. I continued banging on the door and also now shouted for the guard, whom I could laughingly hear saying "We've got a wildcat in there, but we will soon tame her." The women became anxious, fearing punishment and requested that I stopped; so I had no choice and sat down on the floor, staring at the filthy walls of this 6ft. × 10ft. cell. It reminded me of one that I was held prisoner in by the Gestapo in 1944 when I was tortured. Now to be put in a cell again, made me ashamed to have been part of the people who had helped this Allied Occupation.

As time went by, I prayed 'God give me patience' . . . . or was it that God helped those that help themselves? With that firmly in mind I began shouting again for the guard to open the cage. To my amazement he came, opened the door and said: "You come, the captain will see you now."

It was 2 a.m. in the morning; it was cold and I was shivering, both with fear and anger, as he lead me to a small room in which he told me to sit.

As I sat down, a floodlight suddenly shone on my face, which I instinctly shielded with my hands. This took me right back to the days of interrogation by the Gestapo.

These Russians were supposed to be our Liberators, yet they used the same tactics that we had fought so hard to depose. It took all my courage not to be intimidated, so I collected my wits together and shouted in Russian: "Is this supposed to be the third degree? If you are the KGB, you can forget it, tactics like these will get you nowhere. I did not tell the Germans what they wanted to know, even under torture, so I will most certainly not tell anything to you lot. How dare you?"

The floodlight went off and the room light came on. When I removed my hands from my face I found that I was seated opposite an astonished looking man who after some time introduced himself as the captain. I did not give him the opportunity to ask me anything but immediately demanded in Russian, that he telephoned the headquarters at St. Michael to verify, who I was. I explained that I was working there as a translator, nearly adding that on top of that, I was the general's mistress. But I could see that I had already put the fear of God into him when I said that I worked solely for General Potkorny.

As he made no attempt to pick up the phone, in anger I picked it up myself pointing it at him shouting: "Will you ring or must I do it myself?"

The captain, now very agitated, pointed out that it was the middle of the night and that the general would not be pleased to be disturbed. I swiftly replied that his anger would be nothing compared to the heads that would roll if he kept me in here overnight, as the general would be more displeased if he found that these people had detained me from my work for him.

The captain was obviously torn between risking the general's anger, now over the telephone or in the morning when he might have to face him in person. He offered me a cigarette to stall me, but I declined as I didn't smoke anyway and kept on insisting. Finally the captain gave in and asked the operator to put him through to St. Michael.

When he got through, I could here Sacha's booming voice shouting at him: "Put the girl on the receiver . . . . at once."

He obeyed and reached me the receiver, "Where are you my *darughia*?" asked Sacha.

"In jail" I replied with indignation.

"Have you been drinking too much vodka?" he asked jokingly.

This made me even more angry and I replied: "I wish I had, but I will tell you what, I will kill someone if I'm not released at once, then they will have a real reason for keeping me here."

There was a pause, followed by Sacha trying to calm me down as he said: "Don't do it yet, wait till I have arrived . . . . I still want you with me here not in Siberia." He told me to hand him back to the captain, who was now as white as a sheet.

Trembling, he held the receiver and all I could hear was "da, da, da General".

Sacha arrived after an hour to collect me, and I could sense an explosive quality in the air as the general ushered the captain into an adjoining room. Loud exchanges could be heard and Sacha appeared alone to enquire if I was alright? I immediately replied that I was fine now, but that he must go to the cell where I was held, and get the other five women out of there, who had committed no worse a crime than I and who had been locked in there without sanitary facilities and without a woman warder, under conditions worse than any animal had to endure.

Sacha could see that I was not going to be appeased until he did as I asked and so acquiesced to my wish.

When he returned from the cell, he too was a whiter shade of pale, no doubt caused by the stench in there. He immediately summoned the two guards who stood in front of him like iron statues, giving them orders to release the women at once.

I immediately felt better, and Sacha offered me his arm saying: "Let's get out of here."

I took his arm gratefully and fell asleep in the back of the car during the journey home.

When we arrived home at the villa, Sacha could see how exhausted I was and wished me a good-night without questioning me further.

The following day I explained everything and promised faithfully never to venture out again without a pass.

A couple of weeks passed without further incident. Then one day Sacha informed me that a new aid would be arriving in the next two days, a Major Vasily, whom he wished to be included in his birthday guest list.

It was now July the 3rd, an extra special day, Sacha's fortieth birthday. He had gone out very early in the morning, riding his thoroughbred chestnut mare called Nadia.

Frau Koeller and I were out in the garden collecting flowers, when he arrived back, brimming with laughter. "Why are you laughing?" I enquired.

"Because I am happy. I am forty years old today and still alive. That's why I'm laughing" he replied.

I wished him many happy returns of the day, and he dismounted to kiss me. Frau Koeller handed him some flowers, which he promptly gave to his aid, who was also unsure of what he should do with them. To save any further embarrassment, I diverted their attention, by asking Sacha if I might ride his horse down the road and back.

"If she will let you Malinka," was his reply with a broad grin on his face.

So I mounted the mare, but she reared up in an instant and threw me off, much to Sacha's amusement. Trying not to show how much I hurt, I jumped to my feet, but walked rather stiffly towards the door, with Sacha shouting after me: "Shall I come and give you a massage, Malinka, my darling?"

I could see Frau Koeller laughing her head off, so I slammed the door, to show them what I thought of their fun.

The big party was not for some hours yet, which gave me time to nurse my bruises and sort out something to wear, that would hide them.

By the time evening came, I felt a lot better and decided on a red silk Kossack-style dress with a black belt and black braiding on the shoulders.

I asked Frau Koeller what she thought of my appearance and she replied: "I have never had children of my own, but if I had a daughter like you, I should be very proud of her."

We had both spent the afternoon setting out the dinner-table with the finest china and glassware, accompanied by all the silver cutlery we could find. One final glance had met with both our approval at the splendid looking result. I knew that Sacha would be pleased, for he was a perfectionist in everything. Thus, we had made an all out effort to anticipate his every wish.

All that remained for me to do, was one final check in the long mirror upstairs of my own appearance, and so I rushed up the staircase to do just that, when Herr Koeller announced the arrival of our first guests. So I hurriedly made my way back downstairs to greet the first arrivals.

As I stood in the hall-way anticipating the usual officers, there suddenly appeared in the doorway, the most handsome Russian officer I had ever seen. He stood there dressed in a long black leather coat, his cap in his hand, almost taking my breath away.

He had a most captivating smile, and running his fingers through his blond wavy hair asked: "And who do you belong to, my little beauty?"

As he came towards me, rather startled I was about to say 'to no-one' when the other door into the hall opened and the general appeared, saying at the top of his voice: "Comrade Major, I am afraid this one is exclusively reserved for me." To endorse his words, Sacha put his arms around me and continued jokingly:

"But you are still invited to my party tonight."

Major Vasily saluted smartly, but defiantly said as he passed me, "And I trust I will see you again."

After this remark, one could almost see the sparks flying in the air. Sacha however accompanied his new aid to show him where to go, and I returned to my place by the front door to welcome the next arrivals. I was just in time to shake hands with the next guest in fact and almost had my hands shaken off by the enthusiastic greetings.

When everyone had arrived, Frau Koeller announced that dinner was ready to be served, and we all made our way to the lavishly decorated dining area. To my surprise, I realised that Sacha had rearranged the place cards. He had moved his now, former aid, to the other end of the table, seating the new chap, Major Vasily, right opposite me. Sacha seated himself at the head of the table in a gold brocade almost throne-like carver chair, and was thus flanked by me on one side and Major Vasily on the other. I assumed that Sacha had done this on purpose to test my metal, as the saying goes. It was obvious that Major Vasily and I could not avoid eye contact across the table all night. As Sacha was scrutinising my every reaction, I felt sure that he had done this to examine my loyalty. However, Major Vasily took not a blind bit of notice and blatantly flirted with me, and it took all my cunning to avoid a major clash.

At that moment two Russian waiters then filled all our glasses with vodka and Sacha rose to his feet, and to my astonishment made a terrible mistake by toasting me first, then Stalin and then his officers. He downed the drink in one, flung the glass into the fireplace and ordered the waiter to fill another. He noted my disapproving look, but still shouted at the top of his voice: "To you, drink up my beloved."

Fraternisation, as long as it was undertaken with some degree of discretion was one thing, but to openly flaunt me as his mistress, was quite another. It was no wonder, that Sacha's toast, was followed first, with uncertain looks in his direction and then with utter silence.

Sacha, who obviously was beyond caring, immediately ordered another vodka, which he drank down, again in one go, then crushed the glass with his bare hand. Whether he had done this deliberately, to show anyone who dared to oppose him what their possible fate might be, I don't know, but it certainly had the desired effect.

As blood trickled onto the nicely white starched table-cloth, he glared at his guests, shouting almost challengingly: "If anyone does not like it here, they may leave now, before we start on the food.''

The atmosphere was electric, the silence deafening, yet no-one got up. Thus, the general, after carefully studying each and everyone of his guests, summoned Frau Koeller to bring in the food.

I pointed to his still bleeding hand, but he dismissed my concern with a waft of his hand and wrapped a serviette around it.

Realising, that Sacha was in a belligerent mood, I sought to divert his attention by engaging Major Vasily in a conversation, by enquiring about his war record, as he was highly decorated and wore almost as many medals as Sacha. Vasily promptly responded by giving the general a detailed account about how his tank regiment smashed through the German lines and inflicted heavy losses. This now had defused a potentially dangerous situation, and at the same time broken the ice between the major and Sacha.

I, however, got fed up with all the serious war talk, and lightened the tone of the conversation by relating the organ and goat story, which brought the whole table out in laughter.

As the evening progressed, the drinking got heavier, and all our guests became intoxicated and merry.

By 10 p.m., the dinner was over. To my horror, Sacha just pulled off the table-cloth, sending everything that was on it crashing to the floor. This was no party trick, that had accidentally gone wrong. I could see that this had been done deliberately, to show me who, was master in this house. I, however, did not rise to the bait, and remained calm.

After waiting for some seconds for my reaction, Sacha stalked out of the dining-room into the lounge, ordering the waiters to clear up the mess.

What could I say? I quickly ushered everyone else into the lounge and put some Johann Strauss music onto the gramophone.

Sacha immediately came over and took it abruptly off demanding ''Fiery music, Hungarian music, anything, but not those German tunes.''

I could clearly see that he was drunk, and decided that it was best in the interest of peace, to humour him.

He finally found a record that suited his mood, and he made me dance with him, almost violently, to the clapping hands of his comrades! By now, they too, were beyond caring.

Sacha ordered more vodka!

I begged him to stop, but he pushed me aside, flinging the full glass across the room.

Frau Koeller bent over to pick up the pieces, cutting her hands in the process.

I intervened and helped her, which really got Sacha into a rage, and he shouted: "You are the general's woman, not a servant, having to clean up broken glass." And to make his point, he threw another glass against the wall.

Frau Koeller looked frightened and did not know what to do for the best, but I had seen enough. My temper was roused . . . . I had not been in the Resistance for five years, only to be intimidated now, just because he was a general. So I faced Sacha square on, and exclaimed in my very best Russian: "You are a Hero of the Soviet Union, yet you behave like a maniac; I regret that I have fought in the Resistance to rid ourselves of the Germans, because you as their replacement, are not a great deal better. Do you understand?"

Sacha looked furious. So much so, that Major Vasily stepped in front of me, to protect me. The general glared at me over Vasily's shoulders, swayed and sat down with a grin on his face. Vasily withdrew quietly into the background and the general motioned me to come closer. He then complimented me on my Russian pronunciation, but added, that he could not permit me to criticise him, in front of his comrades.

The others came closer, so as not to miss one word of this lusty confrontation. Sacha, however, soon backed down, as he was in no state to retaliate.

To save face, I stormed out of the room before I really said something, I might regret later.

Frau Koeller persuaded me to go back into the room, to make peace, as with tears streaming down her face, she said: "It's the Russian custom to smash glasses, I am only a poor old woman, but I want to live and have enough food to eat. If you don't go back in there, what will happen to my husband and I? He only hired us to look after you?"

This made me think. The vital difference between Frau Koeller and I was, that I was young, and that the general wanted me, body and soul. However, I heeded her words, and all was forgiven, after all it was his birthday! So I went back, restoring peace by offering to sing a few songs.

Major Vasily immediately offered to accompany me on the piano.

As I feared a renewal of conflict with Sacha, I suggested that Comrade Anatoly, should play for me.

Sacha waved his arms wildly in the air and shouted: "I don't care who plays the piano, as long as he plays it well."

Major Vasily took up the challenge, playing Lizt's 'Liebestraum' to perfection.

Everyone gathered around the piano and applauded, with the exception of Sacha, who was too drunk to get up.

Vasily then asked me what I would like to sing, and I gave him the sheet music of my favourite song and began: "*Eine Frau wird erst schön durch die Liebe . . . . . . ganz allein nur . . . . . durch die Liebe . . . .* ". "A woman becomes beautiful, when she is in love . . . . completely in love . . . . ". "*Ach wenn es ewig so bliebe . . . . nur die Liebe . . . . macht erst schön . . . . . .* ". "Oh, if it only would last forever . . . . because love alone . . . . is all that matters . . . . ".

Whilst he was playing for me, I could feel a mutual bond forming and through the music we were transferred into another world, one of beauty and romance. I finished the song amid tumultuous applause and requests for more, but I was exhausted and bade them 'sing for me!'

Thus, Sacha's guests, lead by Major Vasily, began singing a well-known 'Wolga' song. The words were beautiful indeed — their faces lit up with pride of their country, and the memories of loved ones, could be seen in their eyes. The music was very moving and Frau Koeller and I just listened in awe, as a rather turbulent day, drew to a lovely end.

I thanked both Herr and Frau Koeller for their efforts, explaining that the cleaning up should wait till morning. When they had left, also other officers came to bid me good-night, saluting smartly and thanking me. The general was helped to his room by his batman, who then also bade me good-night.

The last to leave was Major Vasily and I opened the door for him, but he forcefully shut it, by placing his large frame against it. He then took me into his arms, and kissed me.

To my own astonishment, I did not struggle, as in my mind, I had already picked him out as the very man, to make Steiner jealous!!

When he released me, curiosity had got the better of me, and I asked: "What would you do if Sacha found out?"

With a grin, his instant reply was: "Don't you know that forbidden fruit, always tastes sweeter?"

Before I could say anything else, the door had opened, and shut behind him. As I was now alone in the hall, I turned off the lights and made my way upstairs. I could not help but smile about Vasily. Although, he was extremely sensual, and would probably make most women weak at the knees, for me, to fall in love with him, would take a good deal more. But one thing was certain, he would be the perfect playmate, to bring Steiner under my spell.

The next day was taken up with a troop inspection at the University Town of Leoben, which was 25 km away. I only saw Sacha briefly before he went and noticed that he looked a little worse for wear, much in contrast to his lively new aid, Major Vasily, who cheekily waved from the car. In fact with Vasily's appointment there appeared to be a new wind blowing through the entire HQ in St. Michael. This was reflected in the much lesser use of the word 'Da', which was previously the most common sound echoing around the walls.

My own workload at HQ was now much reduced, as I had managed to sort out many of the difficulties that had first beset the people of my village. The criteria of concern at HQ became now, the tracking down of war criminals and my involvement was only, as an interpreter.

With so much more time on my hands, Sacha suggested that I took up my riding again. Indeed the day after the big inspection at Leoben, we, Sacha, Vasily, Alexi and I, decided that we would ride to St. Stefan and visit my mother.

It was a hot summer's day and we chose the scenic route, through picturesque woodlands to get there. About half-way through our journey, I noticed two Russian soldiers on horseback pulling behind them a civilian, with a rope around his neck.

As they came nearer, I recognised the man on the rope to be the former Gendarmerie Inspector, who had been a fanatical Nazi supporter! He had been the last man to threaten me with a revolver, before the end of the war, in April 1945, when just like now, I had been on horseback! Then I was an escapee on the run, in fact on my way home, to my sick mother in Lobning.

At that time, he made me dismount from my horse and said: "Your galavanting days are over, and if I shoot you now, not a cockerel, will crow for you."

What a reversal of fate, that we should meet again, and most of all, under such circumstances.

As we drew level, the general halted the soldiers.

The prisoner fell to his knees in front of me, saying: "Please Madam, help me."

Upon which the general demanded to know, who he was?

I then explained the full story, adding that he only let me go, when I reminded him that the Allies were on our doorsteps, and that he would be tried as a war criminal.

Sacha moved his horse close to the prisoner, who was about to get to his feet and brought his riding crop sharply down on his shoulders, to stop him from doing so.

I quickly intervened and begged Sacha to instruct the soldiers to remove the rope from around his neck, but to tie his hands and let the soldiers take him to jail in a civilised way.

To my astonishment, Sacha agreed, and told the guards to remove the man from his sight.

Sacha then galloped ahead of us and I had the feeling that he wanted to divorce himself from the stark reality and ugliness, that this war had brought. Giving orders was one thing, but seeing them carried out in cold blood, was quite another matter.

This incident somehow spoilt the rest of the day. The thing that then completely ruined it for me, was that my mother was not very well. Sacha immediately agreed that I could ride again to see her, but not alone and he assigned, Major Vasily to be my protector.

I awoke the next morning with a tingle of excitement at the prospect of Major Vasily's company. My inner thoughts were twofold! — Vasily versus Steiner.

I switched on the radio as usual, to hear the 8 o'clock news; I was just dressing when Sacha dashed into my room without knocking. He kissed me, and gave me a food parcel to take to my mother. He then walked around me like a ringmaster, saying in a teasing voice: "I am taking a long last look at you, before I let you go with Vasily to St. Stefan."

At that moment a waltz started to play on the radio, with someone singing rather aptly: "Why has every springtime only one May, and why can this silly heart not remain faithful?"

I got hold of Sacha and made him dance with me, more as a concealment of my excitement, than any real desire for a dance, as I had no wish to arouse his suspicion.

Sacha nevertheless said as he left: "You little devil, you had better behave yourself."

I looked over the balcony, and watched him drive off with his ontourage, waving.

Whilst, I was standing there, my mind was already breakfasting on the most poignant questions: "Why on earth, did I hanker after Steiner?" "How deeply was I involved with Sacha?" "Why was I so looking forward to this game with Vasily?"

No sooner had Sacha's car disappeared from sight, when Vasily brought along two beautiful horses. Seeing me standing on the balcony, he pretended to be Romeo. He attempted to climb the trellises, much to my amusement, but gave up, as the frail woodwork was about to give way, to his impressive frame.

I hurried downstairs, rather like Juliet eagerly, only to land in Vasily's open arms. Reluctantly I pulled myself free, and mounted my horse, galloping ahead of him. My instincts told me to put a distance, between the watchful eyes of my golden cage and the uninhabited countryside ahead.

Vasily soon caught up with me and brought my horse to a standstill! We were already on the path to St. Stefan and out of sight. For a few minutes there was complete silence as we rode side by side, glancing at each other guiltily. It suddenly dawned on me, that I was inviting a new and dangerous liaison — which could only lead to disaster. Yet, the man next to me was so provocatively handsome, that I could not resist temptation.

As we approached a clearing in the wood, Vasily suggested a rest and helped me to dismount. We were sandwiched between the two horses, and Vasily took this opportunity to kiss me passionately and I did not stop him, but ran my fingers through his silky blond hair.

Vasily tied both horses to a tree and we sat down on a patch of soft moss, and all my good intentions took wing and vanished. There I was with this masculine, bronzed hunk of a man, whose teeth were as evenly shaped as his forehead, his smiling blue eyes acting like a magnet and drawing my face closer to his.

We looked at each other, for a long while, until Vasily broke the spell by moving and encircling me in his arms, at the same time placing me gently underneath him on the soft moss, saying in a husky voice: "You are much too beautiful and much too dangerous, but I don't give a damn about the consequences."

Fearing that I had allowed myself to become too involved, too quickly, I put my hand over his mouth, and told him that my heart was not free.

To which he asked "Is it Sacha?"

My reply was honest as I said: "No it's Steiner, a partisan hero, who has captured my heart."

He sat up and said: "Why aren't you with him then?"

So I explained that he had a Russian girl-friend, a woman doctor named Olga Petrovich.

Vasily jumped to his feet and laughed.

When I asked why, he said: "She is known to quite a few officers, distributing her favours."

This revelation shook me to the core, and completely altered my views of Steiner. There I had been placing him on a pedestal, when he should really have been more at home in the gutter. Anger welled up inside of me, at my own stupidity, and I was determined to get my own back on him.

I got to my feet and Vasily closed his arms around me, gently saying: "I will wipe the picture of this Steiner, completely out of your mind."

He kissed my face all over, his soft lips gently brushing my eyes, my nose and cheeks, as if to remove all traces of Steiner's presence forever. Although, he did actually vanish from my mind momentarily, he was quickly replaced by Sacha's image.

We sat down, and Vasily said that now that all was settled, there were only the two of us to worry about. But I interrupted and asked: "What about Sacha?"

He arrogantly replied: "I can deal with him as well, all I need is to be very discreet."

I was swept away on a wave of optimism that I had not encountered since before the war, as Vasily kissed me into oblivion!

When we finally stopped kissing I couldn't help but to explain that there was nothing sexual between the general and I, lest he should think that I was another Olga.

He replied: "Oh you silly little girl, don't you think that I know this?"

With this new understanding between us we mounted our horses and proceeded to St. Stefan to see my mother.

My mother was extremely pleased to see me and absolutely astonished that Sacha had given me such a handsome escort. We stayed for about an hour and then began the homeward journey, back to the golden cage.

We stopped at the same spot and dismounted, walking the horses side by side, as if to prolong the few precious moments, that from now on would have to be guarded carefully.

Vasily seemed very philosophical about us. When I reminded him again about the dangers involved in such a clandestine love affair, he replied laughingly: "I know, I can never marry you under present regulations, but Stalin can't prevent me from loving you, my beautiful girl — I fought for Russia and was prepared to die for my country, but I must be allowed to live a life of my own choosing."

We arrived at the villa rather subdued, to a boisterous reception from Sacha, who had awaited our return eagerly, although he asked us if we enjoyed the ride, the hostile look he gave Vasily, said it all.

After a smart salute, Vasily excused himself and left me in the hands of Sacha, who escorted me to my room. He searched my face for possible signs of guilt. However I was not going to be intimidated, and began telling him how well the horse, his mare, Nadia, had behaved.

He quickly replied: "I know that the horse would behave, but did you my *darughia*?" He firmly pulled me into his arms and kissed my neck. I surrendered, with my eyes closed, and a distinct feeling of repulsion, as Vasily's tender kisses were still lingering in my mind.

Sacha's voice brought me back to reality, as he reminded me to be punctual at his table for dinner.

I smiled graciously, so as not to arouse suspicion and went to dress.

As I changed for dinner, my anxiety grew, with fears that over dinner I would be seated opposite Vasily, who would undoubtedly flirt and give the game away. As I walked down the staircase, I determined to be as good an actress, as Lucy Koerting had trained me to be, in order to shield Vasily from Sacha's wrath of jealousy.

Lucy would have been proud of my performance, as I swept into the dining-room, in a demure black dress which gave me a prim and proper image. Before taking my seat, I made a point of kissing Sacha on his lips, cordially greeting the other guests.

But when I was seated, Sacha sarcastically remarked "I didn't expect you to be buttoned up like a nun." He flashed a crafty look in the direction of Vasily, who just grinned from ear to ear.

It was then that I realised that I had gone too far in compensating for my guilty conscience. This dinner party was the most subdued occasion that I had ever participated in. It was only the customary smashing of glasses, that brought any flicker of life to it.

The following days were to become the most dramatic in my life, as I entered a new arena of confronation, suddenly over self-conscious, of everything I did and said. I knew that I would have to use all my feminine wiles, and all my acting ability to avert a bloody outcome.

Vasily, however, seemed undeterred. He arranged clandestine meetings at the oddest times and in the oddest places when he hoped that the general was out on duty, or busy with some official functions.

One day, he even had the audacity to come to my room in the middle of the day, when he knew that Sacha was on some official meeting, miles away. Just as he was as usual declaring his great love for me, the door opened and Herr Koeller appeared with his automatic rifle ready to confront the intruder. Vasily, who had already removed his shirt, was now faced with the in comparison tiny Herr Koeller, brandishing his automatic rifle, pointing straight into his chest.

To my astonishment, Vasily, casually took the rifle off the Austrian and smilingly remarked: "The war is over, you had better go back to your wife and protect her if you think that there is going to be a revival of fighting."

Herr Koeller, bewildered by what he saw, explained that he was under orders from the general to protect me from any intruders.

I intervened by saying: "It's alright Herr Koeller, he is not an intruder, he is here on official business."

In total disbelief, utter confusion and without his rifle, Herr Koeller withdrew.

Vasily collapsed in laughter and said: "Only a woman in love could utter such an irrational answer." He picked me up and flung me onto the bed, as the telephone rang. Without thinking, Vasily picked it up. The smile soon vanished from his face, as I heard him say: "Da, Da, General."

When he replaced the receiver, he explained that the general had forgotten some papers and that he would take them at once.

When I asked how he knew that he was here, he just smiled and said that he had told the girl at HQ that he was here on official business, doing an inventory of the foodstocks in the house, as had been requested by the general some days ago. He kissed me once more, and putting on his shirt in a teasing manner said: "You had better give the rifle back to the pip-squeak, because he will have to protect you from any other officers, on 'official' business." When he was dressed, he saluted me in a clowning fashion and left.

On another occasion, we met behind a large tree hoping that it would shield our bodies from view. It was all so romantic, this wild infatuation which Vasily interpreted, as a great love. Yet, deep inside of me I knew that I was still hankering after Karl Steiner.

Rather strangely Vasily reiterated phrases of love in his native language which were only too common to me. But the fact that this georgeous and brave officer from another world should desire me with such passion, made it impossible to sever myself from him. Love indeed can have many faces, and can become a paradise, or a living hell. The latter I wished desperately to avoid.

There was another occasion, on which we arranged to meet in the stables. It was actually too close to home for me, but I agreed nevertheless as Vasily always managed to dispell my misgivings somehow.

Whilst shutting the stable doors behind me, my nose became acutely aware of the strong perfume of another woman. The only other woman who frequented the stables and who actually wore perfume, was Olga Petrovich.

I expressed my suspicions to Vasily who immediately dismissed them, by saying: "You are imagining danger everywhere, but it seems strange to me that you don't seem to realise, that I am the only danger here."

This made me smile at my own nature and I began to doubt my overzealous mind. As usual I had to stand on my tiptoes to kiss Vasily. But this time, he picked me up and stood me on a straw bundle saying: "Is that better now my little detective?"

We both burst out laughing and wound up in the hay. Although we were only playing with each other . . . . . fooling around as the popular phrase goes, Vasily startled me with his profoundness when he said: "The only paradise we cannot be banished from, is that which exists in our mind." And as if he had a premonition, he added: "I will always remember you the way you are now."

Although I was in a state of bliss, at the back of my mind was the ever watchful little policeman carefully guarding against the final act of love-making. And as I could see that Vasily was again getting far too serious, I quickly redirected his mind off his physical desires, with my quirky sense of humour.

Moments later, I heard the back stable door slam, but again Vasily insisted that I was imagining things.

But this time, I felt sure that someone had been watching us, and my fears could not even be stilled by his funny comments. I got to my feet, covered in hay and straw, much to the amusement of Vasily, whose laughter at the sight of me was so infectious, that I could not help but join in. He picked all the bits of straw off me whilst I remarked, that I could easily pass as a scarecrow! This set him off again, as to my dismay he heartily agreed.

We decided to leave separately. When I resembled my former self, I ventured back the way I had come, literally sneaking back into my rooms. As I shut my bedroom door, an old proverb came to mind . . . . about shutting the stable door, after the horse had bolted. But as my mind was carelessly wandering through unknown pastures, my eyes caught a fleeting glimpse of myself in the mirror. This brought me back instantly to the present moment. As the time was fast approaching dinner, I quickly changed, so as to appear the vision of perfection, that Sacha was as always expecting me to be.

Several days passed with Vasily and I only exchanging fleeting glances, under the increasingly watchful eyes of Sacha. The worst thing was, that we did not even get a moment alone to arrange another rendezvous.

One morning, after Frau Koeller had placed the breakfast tray on my side-table in my bedroom, she remarked: "Is the General ill? I heard him summon the doctor to his HQ office over the telephone."

"When?" I nonchalantly asked.

"Oh, he phoned before he left here and asked her to be at his office for 11 a.m."

A quick glance at the clock confirmed that I would have at least an hour to get ready and go there. I thanked Frau Koeller for the tray and pretended that it was probably some boring official business matter, as he would surely have asked her to the villa if he had felt ill.

Frau Koeller considered the matter for a little while and agreed that it could be nothing serious. She then wished me a good morning and left me to enjoy my breakfast.

Little did she know, of course the matter was serious. I immediately put two and two together, realising full well why Olga was summoned. She was probably Sacha's spy.

I rushed into my clothes, gulped down some of my breakfast and decided to go and investigate.

When I reached HQ I was a little later than the appointed hour, but I was happy in the knowledge, that Olga would already be with Sacha, as she was never late on official business. As I approached the long corridor to his office, I took off my shoes and sneaked right up to his door. I could hear Olga's high-pitched voice as clear as a bell, relating my rendezvous with Vasily, almost word for word.

Sheer terror made me shake all over when Sacha's booming voice ended the conversation by saying that he would deal with this matter personally and that she was now to give him the report about the hospital that he had asked her for.

Absolutely terrified, I fled back to the villa, as my worst fears had been confirmed. I went back to my room and just sat there motionless.

When the phone rang in the early afternoon, I knew exactly which bell was tolling. A few moments later Frau Koeller appeared and informed me that Sacha had requested my immediate presence at HQ. It took every ounce of courage for me to pretend, that I was unaware of what was going on.

I walked to the HQ like a man who was going to keep an appointment with his hangman, but decided that the best policy was to deny everything.

Sacha asked me to be seated and to my amazement, came straight to the point, accusing me of having an affair with Major Vasily.

By then it had crossed my mind that the best form of defence was always attack. So I got to my feet and said almost indignantly, "Who says so?"

Sacha swiftly replied: "Dr Petrovich left me in no doubt as to the goings on behind my back." He clenched his fists, bringing them down hard on the table, shouting at me: "How dare you deceive me, you little Austrian devil, after all I have done for you and your family?"

I kept my cool and replied: "Perhaps, before you condemn me, you would like to hear my side of this story?"

Sacha was visibly taken aback at my calm composure and allowed me to speak. So I told him that Olga was well known for distributing her favours, and that having been rejected by Vasily, she had no doubt decided to revenge herself at someone else's expense. And I quoted the old saying to him: 'Hell hath no fury like a woman scorned'.

Sacha's face relaxed and he came around his desk, embracing me and kissing me, and I was almost sure that I had managed to convince him. Little did I realise that he merely lulled me into a false sense of security.

I went back to the villa, and dressed myself extremely elegantly for dinner, hoping to create a harmonious atmosphere between Sacha, Vasily and I.

However when I approached the dining-room with all the officers seated, including Sacha, there was only one empty chair, the one opposite mine, Vasily's. Although, fearing the worst, but in order not to arouse any further suspicion, I casually enquired if Major Vasily was late.

Sacha had only been waiting for me to ask as his reply was instantaneous: "It's most unfortunate, but he has been posted to Vienna." The triumphant look on his face which had obviously been intended to humble me for my indiscretion, and the deliberate punishment of leaving the empty chair as a reminder to look at across the table, all added to breaking my composure, and tears began streaming down my face.

At this moment of truth, I did not care what Sacha thought, or would do to me. I just sat there, leaving my food untouched, staring at my plate.

There was a deadly silence as all that could be heard were the knives and forks of the eating guests. No-one dared to say anything.

Sacha, finally broke the silence by saying very quietly to me: "I thought you were a woman and not a malinka, so act like one."

I shot to my feet, picked up my glass and said defiantly: "A toast to the great Russian General, Alexander Potpokorny, a true Hero of the Soviet Union." I downed my glass in one go, smashed it against the wall and left. I went to my room and flung myself onto my bed and cried without restraint.

A few moments later, Frau Koeller came into my room, for the first time without knocking, and sat herself next to me on the bed saying: "For God's sake girl think, as long as the general is governing here, he will not set you free. My husband and I have discussed this, and we are certain that the general is genuinely, deeply in love with you.''

I turned around and screamed at her: "But I am not in love with him, so what do you want me to do now?''

She replied: "Play it by ear, be patient, the occupation cannot last forever. You are young enough to start a new life, when this is all over, think about it, you are luckier than most, you even have a talented voice and will have no problem in making singing your career.''

She kissed my hand and that small gesture touched my heart. I began to realise that Frau Koeller was right and that the only option left to me was to play this hand out to the bitter end.

I went to the bathroom, washed my face and calmed down, still wondering what had really happened to Vasily? Would he really always remember me? At this point Sacha entered, also without knocking, looking arrogant, but drunk. He removed his revolver and flung it onto my bed.

The thought had crossed my mind, so I said: "If you want to use it, do it now and get it over with.''

He almost pounced on me, grabbed me by the shoulders and said: "I hoped that by now, you would have come to your senses and realised how much I really love you. So much so, that I defied the KGB and Stalin's orders by helping you and your friends. Doesn't that count for anything? The least you owe me is loyalty.''

He now held me so close that I could hardly breathe and I began to feel like a rag doll in his powerful arms. All the strength had gone out of my body, as I was emotionally exhausted. He kissed and kissed me, but without response, until he finally sat me on a chair and said: "I will leave you now to think things over, but know this, I swear that I will take you with me wherever I am posted whether you want to come or not. And you never know, I may have enough influence with Stalin, to even get permission to marry you. But rest assured, even if that fails you will still be coming with me, as my mistress.'' And as he left the room, he added: "You will be mine, you belong to me.''

This was the finale for me, I now felt ill with terror. A caged animal could not have felt worse. I knew now that it would only be a matter of time before Sacha would force me into his bed. His declarations of love had turned into an obsession. My greatest fear was not of sleeping with him, but that of becoming pregnant. If that was ever to happen, then all was lost, my singing career would definitely be extinguished overnight, chaining me to a man I had once been fond of, but whom I had now grown to fear. I made up my mind, then and there, that I would not go willingly to meet such a fate.

Surprisingly, I did not see anything of Sacha over the next few days, which gave me time to think and scheme. But even that did not help, as my mind went round in circles.

Then on the fourth day of my solitude, Sacha suddenly came to ny room in the morning, but only to inform me that his next)osting was in Vienna and that we would be leaving the following lay.

Acute panic set in, as I was still unsure of what I should do.

The day of departure arrived all too soon and still no concrete plan for escape had materialised in my mind.

After breakfast, Sacha suddenly announced that he had his car standing by to take me to my mother. For a split second I thought that he had decided to let me go, but no such luck. He quickly added that I could not possibly go to Vienna without saying goodbye to my mother. Still in a daze at this unexpected news, he immediately shocked me further by explaining that he had entrusted Steiner of all people, with the task of taking me there and ensuring my safe return by 8 p.m.

Although I trembled at the very thought of being let out of Sacha's sight for a few hours, I nevertheless made a fuss of him as we left, so as not to arouse suspicion.

Slowly but surely, the heavy cloud that had been over my head lifted. This process had probably been much aided by the sight of Steiner. Even after all, that Vasily had told me, deep down, I had not been able to erase my own private obsession for Steiner.

As we were sitting side by side, with Steiner driving, I could feel his eyes on me. Pretending to be without a care in the world, I casually glanced in his direction and caught him. When our eyes met for seconds only, it sent hot and cold shivers down my spine, awaking my senses from the battering they had received over the last few days.

After two and a half kilometres of silence, Steiner suddenly pulled the car into a woody lay-by, switched off the engine, bent over me and kissed me. "That is what you have wanted me to do for a long time . . . isn't it?" he said.

I was so startled, that I smacked his face. He just laughed, so I responded sarcastically saying: "I expected a kiss from you to be far more exciting . . . . what's the matter? Has Olga exhausted you?"

I had gone a little too far. Karl retaliated by smacking my face hard. Upon seeing me wince in pain, he instantly took me into his arms saying: "How could I do such a thing?" He held me close and passionately explained: "If you think that Olga is my lover, you are barking up the wrong tree. I only used her as a smoke-screen to hide my real feelings for you, from the general.'' He then told me that when he realised how many people depended for help on my relationship with Sacha, it became imperative to stay away as the needs of a one, must definitely be sacrificed for the needs of the many.''

'Very noble,' I thought.

And he added ''I would have gone to any length to stand by my ideals, even to make you hate me, if necessary.''

'Such integrity is rare,' I thought, 'no wonder I fell for him.'

Distant noises suddenly made Steiner sit up and we could both see Russian soldiers riding through the wood, shooting at something.

Anxious not to be seen stationary, Karl switched on the engine and moved the car into the undergrowth, where it was camouflaged by the bushes.

I promptly switched the ignition off, looked him straight in the eyes and said ''Why don't we throw our lot in together? We are made of the same material, two fighters . . . . . one cause.''

Steiner replied: ''I am wondering if I have done the right thing here.''

My mind, however, was already way ahead of his, as a plan began to formulate in my mind: 'ESCAPE from SACHA'.

But there was now an added complication, there was also Karl's fate to consider. Wild thoughts were racing through my mind as I was lying in his arms, his dark eyes sinking deep into my heart.

Steiner, oblivious to what I was thinking, continued: ''I need not tell you how beautiful you are . . . you know it yourself . . . . and too many, have said it before me, but no-one could love you more than I do. There is no limit to what I would do for you . . . my dearest.''

He kissed me, but with so much passion, that I nearly passed out.

My mind was now convinced, that he would escape with me to Graz, and that no-one in this world could stop us.

''What thoughts are you conjuring up in that mind of yours?'' he said, as he had been watching my brain go through its paces, my expression changing accordingly.

''Oh nothing special,'' I replied; but my thoughts were already in another region, miles away from here and well out of reach of Sacha and his troops. Free and happy in the knowledge, that the man I loved and desired most, had declared his love for me. I was not dreaming, it was really true. Then suddenly, the image of my mother crossed my mind. Surely the general would not harm an elderly lady, just because I had dared to flee from my golden cage?

I was thinking about these and many other things, yet I had not even mentioned the word 'Escape' to Steiner. Whatever was I thinking of? While I was in this reverie, Karl had decided to drive on, and it was only, when he swerved to avoid something on the road, that I realised that we were nearly at my mother's house.

It was about 3 p.m., and to my delight, we found my mother happy and well, sitting in the garden, reading a book. She was surprised to see me, and glad. Alas, I never got round to telling her the real reason for my visit as she bubbled over with all the local news.

In order to finalise the plan that had been formed in my head, I invented some pretext to get Steiner to come and look at something in the house. My mother was quite happy for me to show him around, and continued with her book.

We entered what had been my private room, glancing at each other as only lovers do. The electricity was flowing through both our bodies and could almost be seen. In a sudden urge of recklessness, Karl locked the door, as if to shut out the rest of the world.

"This is how love should be" he exclaimed.

I replied: "No Karl, not quite like this. I don't want to hide any more. I don't want to go back to the man who holds the trump cards over our heads. I don't want to be handed back to Sacha. Surely there must be another way?"

From the expression on Steiner's face, I could see that finally it had dawned on him what was going through my mind . . . 'ESCAPE'. Little pearls of perspiration emerged on his forehead as the full implications of what I had said sunk in.

As if to buy time, he picked me up and carefully laid me onto the bed. He bent over me, his hot breath fanning my face, as his mind now began working in first gear.

It was now or never for me, and so I said: "Please, let's take this chance of freedom while we can. We have the opportunity, with the general's car to go to Graz without anyone able to stop us. Karl, an opportunity like this will never come again."

He nodded and said: "Alright then, we must leave at once and make for Bruck, but we will have to get petrol from an old friend of mine, who owns the hotel there. With a full tank, we should then make Graz in two hours, and if all goes well, you will be free of the general."

I had every confidence in Karl and off we went, kissing my mother rather hurriedly goodbye.

The first part of our journey was easy and we arrived in Bruck in good time. But that was also where we hit our first snag, i.e. over fuel.

His friend depended on the Russians for his supply, and this was not due until the next morning. To add to this worry, his hotel was full up with Russians, which meant that he couldn't even put us up for the night. He nevertheless insisted that we stayed the night in a little guest-house that he knew. So without any other option open to us, we agreed to stay the night with his friend.

When we got to our room I was beginning to feel the approach of doom, but said laughingly to Karl: "Well never mind what happens, I truly will not object to dying, as there can be no better way to leave this earth than in the arms of the man that you love."

Karl became furious about this and snapped at me: "Don't be silly, the country needs young talents like yours and the whole world lies before your feet."

"But that means nothing to me without your love," I replied.

Steiner just became more agitated and suddenly burst out with the following words: "Do you have any idea, what these Nazi pigs did to me in Wolfsberg? . . . . . They castrated me like an animal and I was the only one of four men, to survive the ordeal. I wish to God I were dead."

I stared at Karl with an expression of absolute horror, my mind being not quite capable of understanding.

"Look for yourself, how the Gestapo butchered me!!" He sat himself on the bed and began to undo his trousers.

Little did Karl realise why he had invoked such terror in me. I had never seen a healthy man naked, never mind a butchered one. I threw myself on top of him to stop him from undressing further.

He mistook this merely as disgust at his actions.

I tried to reason with him, begging him to calm down as the other people staying might overhear us.

But Karl was already beyond my reach. He just screamed at me: "I don't care about the Russians or their damn general, they can all go to hell."

I soon realised that this love of ours lay in tatters, and that the agonising trial of severing emotions with dignity had begun.

One sentence had destroyed what might have been a paradise on earth . . . . "They castrated me like an animal."

This handsome man felt helpless. All my pleading fell on deaf ears as Steiner yelled even louder.

The owner of the guest-house came and knocked on our door, enquiring if there was anything wrong. Karl reached for his revolver.

I closed my eyes saying: "Oh God no, please don't let this happen!"

Karl must have heard me, as he shouted "No nothing is wrong." He took me in his arms and said: "I am sorry, I am just a total failure. First I fuelled your desires for me, making you believe that there was sexual energy and passion in my veins, only because I got so steamed up by your beauty, ... when in reality there is nothing but a shell, and only a butchered one at that."

Feelings of total despair were obviously taking over his mind. Although I began to feel great pity, I knew that it would never do to show it, so I diverted his mind from the torturer within, by asking: "Did you really mean it when you said that you loved me so much that there was no limit to what you would do for me if I asked?"

"Yes. You know I do mean it."

"Prove it then."

"How?" he asked.

"By getting me the hell out of here."

I knew it had been selfish to ask, but what else could I do, it was the only thing that brought him back to reality. Otherwise, he might have ended up killing himself with the depression that seemed to almost totally engulf him.

He calmed himself, and we must have both just fallen asleep, for I woke the next morning still fully dressed, and so was Steiner lying across from me.

We quickly got up, saw his friend, filled the car with petrol, and before another soul was to be seen anywhere, made our way towards Graz.

Steiner drove too fast at times, but I could understood why. It was possible that an all out alert had been issued by the general for our arrest. The sooner we reached our destination, the better.

Common sense replaced our inner moods and problems, only the challenge to succeed remained evident. To my astonishment Karl told me that he would return to St. Michael with the car, to face the fury of Sacha.

When I asked him why, he replied: "He can only shoot me . . . and that will save me doing it myself one day, when I can no longer bear just to exist."

I told him not to even think such rubbish. To my mind we were fighters who had encountered the scum of the earth. We were of a different breed to those who were born after us. They would never have to reach our high standards of loyalty and courage, but would read about people like us in books and marvel at the way we faced death and torture and never gave in. 'Service before Self' . . . . . .

was our motto and always would be.

We reached Graz and my aunt's hideaway, where once more by the light of a flickering candle, I felt safe again.

Karl Steiner said a quick goodbye and drove off without looking back.

I stood there and saluted him as long as the car was in sight and thought: 'THIS PROMISE OF PARADISE . . . . . . ONCE NEARLY WAS MINE . . . . ! ! ! '

Johnny Spitfire

It was now August 1945.

The British troops had followed in the Russian footsteps and occupied the entire Steiermark. Our house had began, with each day passing, to resemble a home again. Glass windows had replaced contraptions of paper and sacking material, and doors were once more hanging properly from their hinges.

The food situation, was the only thing that had not improved. In fact, it was worse than ever with our family struggling, to afford one meal per day. However, the whole atmosphere pervading in our area appeared to be lightened with the departure of the Russian Bear. And Austrian girls could soon be seen, on the arms of British soldiers. Mr Churchill, in his 1942 speech, had promised to liberate us, yet, fraternisation was still officially forbidden.

During these past months, I had resigned myself to a lot of things. I had moved back home to my mother and had firmly decided to leave any thinking to the politicians in the future, and to just put up with whatever fate threw my way.

My foremost concern these days, was my singing career, and my biggest challenge was organising transport for myself to and from Graz, in order to attend my singing lessons.

August was hot, rainy, sticky and lazy; thus, one fine summer's day I decided to go and visit my friend Irma, for a couple of days, at the nearby town of Zeltweg. She earned her living as a tailoress, and owned a bungalow which she had inherited from her husband, who was killed in the war, in 1943.

I arrived in the late afternoon, just escaping an almighty lownpour, as the heavens opened, when I got to Irma's front door. She was pleased to see me and quickly ushered me in. Whilst, taking my coat, she noticed my astonished look at the Royal Air Force uniforms, that were hanging everywhere. She hurriedly explained that she was now working for the British Forces, RAF, and that among her customers she even counted a squadron leader and some other high-ranking officers. She added: "As a matter of fact, I'm expecting a couple of them any moment now."

No sooner had she finished her sentence, than a car could be heard screeching down the road. As we glanced out of the side window by the door, where the rain was now lashing down hard, we saw a vehicle pull up.

"That must be them," said Irma, and before I had time to get out of the way, the door sprung open and two officers rushed past me like a flash of lightning.

I pushed the door to, and as I turned, the squadron leader said laughingly: "Hello there, I am Ralph."

"Ralph who?" I enquired somewhat surprised at their informal entry.

He replied "Ralph Hayes, and this is my friend 'Johnny Spitfire'."

Suddenly, the door flew open with the force of the storm, and Johnny and I rushed to shut it. With his hand on mine, startled, we looked at each other and momentarily time stood still . . . . the boyish looking blond-haired officer smiled helplessly at me, as he spoke breaking the spell. "My christian name is spelled with two nn's."

To which I promptly replied: "Well your surname is quite familiar to me, and needs no explanations."

"Oh indeed," said he, still holding my hand.

My brain echoed, 'Please God No'.

Irma interrupted this little 'tête-a-tête' in a loud voice saying: "Burgi was in the Resistance from 1938 to 45, so she knows all about the planes you are flying."

Ralph got very interested and asked me to tell him more.

However Johnny's face turned white, as he said with all seriousness: "Please don't, not now, the war is over."

"What's wrong with you all of a sudden?" enquired Ralph.

But Johnny chose to ignore him and turning to me, asked me if I spoke English.

"Enough to say yes and no" was my reply, as he wasted no time in replying: "Oh good, I hope that you will say yes, as I would like to invite you to the mess tonight."

His quickness of mind somehow surprised me and I retorted almost in defence: "I thought you had orders not to liaise with the Austrian girls?"

His reply was equally swift as he said: "Our orders are to sort out only those, that are Nazis."

"And do say, how can you tell the difference between those that are, and those that are not?" I replied.

"They are all on file," said he.

I had to laugh about this and he asked me what I thought was funny. So I explained: "By the time that you have looked at a file, you will probably be in love with the girl, and then will it really make any difference whether she is on file?"

"Oh," he said "perhaps I have a lot to learn yet."

Irma brought our debate to a halt by announcing that tea was ready in the kitchen. Johnny gave me his arm and led me into the kitchen, pulling a chair out, he waited for me to be seated, like a true gentleman.

Once again our eyes met head on! I pulled myself together only to see Johnny's hand trembling as he poured my tea, and I wished then and there, that I would have enough courage to get up and go back where I had come from. As the thought had crossed my mind, so the decision was taken out of my hands, by Johnny seating himself close to me on one side and the wall, on the other eliminating any further thoughts of 'escape'.

Ralph sat himself next to Johnny, and started pushing him even closer to me, so that his body was almost crushing me against the wall. Even so, a tingle crept all the way up and down my spine.

"You cannot escape now Fräulein" Johnny said, and I thrilled to the way he pronounced the latter.

Irma joined the conversation saying: "Do you know something, to look at you two, one would think that you had known one another all of your life."

'Perhaps fate was like that' . . . . I thought, . . . 'only we refused to see it at times.'

Ralph and Johnny departed after tea, promising to pick us up at 6 p.m. Irma was bubbling over with ideas, as to what clothes we should wear; but I was wandering in the past as I gazed out of the window at the beautiful rainbow, which had followed the heavy rain.

Almost as if my thoughts had been visible to her, Irma brought me back to the present by saying: "Burgi . . . . are you listening to me . . . . it's no use living in the past, I knew what you were thinking when you saw Johnny."

"Don't be silly, come, just look at the lovely rainbow," I answered in defence of my thoughts!

I was afraid to admit it, she was right, but it was hard to forget, especially when the door to my memory would open, like the sluice of a floodgate, at the sight of a handsome man in uniform.

Irma could sense that I was not prepared to discuss the matter further, and changed the subject back to the matter of clothes. When she had finally satisfied herself, by choosing the right kind of dress for me to wear, she began on my hair, pinning it up and curling it on top. "I've got a *diamanté* clip" she said, and went to fetch it, placing it sideways into my hair, so that it would be more noticeable. At last she considered me attractive enough and stopped fussing, getting herself ready.

We did not have to wait long for the arrival of our escorts. They were punctual, both looking extremely smart and polished. With Johnny driving, we set off for the base at Zeltweg, and Ralph had to constantly remind him to keep his eyes on the road. We laughed and joked and got to the mess with the band music already in full swing. They were playing, 'What is this thing called love?' and Johnny and I joined in.

My mouth began to water as we danced past the delicious looking buffet, and my eyes became transfixed at the sight of all that lovely food. Thankfully, Johnny noticed, and tactfully suggested a rest.

We sat down at a table and he fetched me two plates; one of sandwiches, and one of cakes. Despite his amazement, I ate all that was on them. Obviously Johnny had no idea of the hunger and starvation, that was still rife everywhere, the lack of food had been especially bad in the last six months.

However, even though he was oblivious to the facts, he immediately offered to get some more sandwiches and cake. I whispered into his ear that I had eaten enough, but that I would very much like to take some with me for my mother. Astounded, he agreed, returning with a box filled to the top, which he gently placed into my hands.

Somehow I felt awful, but this was not a time to let pride get in my way.

Johnny told me to think nothing of it, and pulled me up to dance.

'You are my sunshine, my only sunshine' the band played, and everyone joined in singing, although most of them did not know the words, but the tune was delightful.

When we finally sat down, Johnny got a tiny pink dictionary out of his pocket and translated the words for me. Now and then, we laughed at my pronunciation of English and his of German.

Eventually we decided to go for a walk. It was nearly midnight, but the sky was lit with a full moon and an array of stars that were sparkling like a crystal chandelier.

Johnny held my arm and said: "It's difficult to say, what I should like to express."

I was startled that he should chose to use 'bad' language in front of me, and told him so.

He got out the dictionary once again, and laughed like a drainpipe when he realised that I had mistaken the word 'difficult' for the word '*teufel*' which was the German word for devil. He snapped the dictionary shut, and before I knew what was happening, took me in his arms and kissed me, with such passion that I grew afraid that the situation I found myself in would soon reach the point of no return. So I pulled myself free and asked him if he knew the difference between the word love, and the word passion. He gently encircled me in his arms again and asked if we could not discuss this at some other time. But I persisted, freeing myself for a second time and walked over to a wooden bench under a nearby tree and bade him to think about what I had asked.

Johnny finally came over and sat down next to me saying: "To me it seems quite simple. Do you understand how a man and women interact darling?"

"Yes Johnny," I replied.

"Well then you know what it's all about" he said.

To me this was no answer at all to my question and I said so, explaining: "There is a distinct difference; passion to me means sex, and I could not have sex with anyone, unless I was very much in love."

Johnny fell silent and was obviously taken aback by my directness. He then took me by the arm and suggested that we should rejoin the others in the mess.

When we returned to our table, the band announced that the evening had come to an end and Ralph and Irma joined us, so that we could all set off together to make the journey home.

Most noticeable was the hush, that had fallen over all four of us. I had the feeling that both men were disappointed with the evening's venture. They had probably expected Irma and I to be easy pickings.

They dropped us outside Irma's door and swiftly said 'goodnight'. As their car drove up the road like a bat out of hell, Irma and I laughed and went indoors. We were both tired, wished each other a good-night and went straight to bed.

By lunch-time, the next day, I was ready to go back home to St. Stefan, when quite unexpectedly, Johnny turned up in a car.

With a suitcase in my hand, I was just shutting the front door. He jumped over the gate and shouted: "Where are you off to?"

"Home" I replied.

He went frantic, babbling so quickly in English, that I had to ask him to slow right down, as I couldn't understand a word when he talked so fast. He calmed himself and begged me to stay just one more night.

I agreed as his face looked so sincerely unhappy, that I believed his request to be genuine.

He jumped for joy, cleared the gate with one leap again and shouted that he would pick me up at 6 p.m. He then got into the car and drove off, waving.

When his car had disappeared from sight, I picked up my case and went back to the house. When I tried to tell Irma what had happened, she immediately said that there was nothing to explain, and engaged my help with the ironing.

As I ploughed my way through a huge pile of shirts, Irma suddenly said: "That's his shirt you're ironing."

I made no reply and pretended that it was really not worth mentioning, but in the back of my mind, I suddenly realised that I did not want to fall under the spell of this slim, twenty-four-year-old pilot with blond hair, just because my emotions were at a vulnerable low ebb. It also occurred to me that, what Johnny considered to be his ideal standard of love, need not be extended to sex, nor to domesticity on cue. Surely one could be extremely happy for days, even weeks, without ultimate surrender. The largest part of the pleasure for a man, lay after all in the chase, or did it?

There was no use in my asking Irma about matters of this kind, as she considered me "Too highbrow by far" as she always reminded me, that she did not have my upbringing and education, and could not possibly be expected to understand my reasoning.

I was glad, when 6 p.m. came and with it Johnny, who brought me flowers and handed them to me with that little boy lost look, that made him quite irresistible.

When we arrived at the mess hall, Johnny suggested a long walk in the lovely gardens surrounding it, explaining that we would eat later in the mess. But first and foremost he wanted to talk.

"There must be no past, only the future between us," he said as his opening statement, thus eliminating any questions about the past.

I was most impressed and surprised at the morass of entangled emotions that this young man managed to evoke in me.

"You are adorable," he said softly, "I must have been waiting for you to come into my life little girl . . . . . do you understand, what I am saying?"

I nodded.

His lips were gently touching my hair and then trailed over my eyelids, along my cheek-bones . . . . . soon there was no space between our bodies, and I could feel, the hurry of his heartbeat.

"No," I said as if awakening from a dream, "please don't, not now."

The sultry music could be heard from the mess hall . . . . 'Fools rush in . . . where angels fear to tread' and I began humming the melody, to which we both began to dance, with the full moon above us.

My head advised caution, but my heart was thudding with nervous excitement. How can one ever legislate about these things?

And Johnny sang: "So let this love begin, please let this fool rush in." The softness of his voice and the tenderness in his eyes made him irresistible, and I could not help, but want to kiss his inviting lips. I clasped my hands around his neck in anticipation, and he gently bent over and kissed me, like I had never been kissed before.

To me, it seemed that I was always listening to my instincts rather than my intellect when a new phase of my life was about to begin. It was either euphoria . . . . or emotional conflict, but certainly never dull. And so it was this time, but somewhere in the dark recesses of my heart, was still a picture of Steiner.

Whenever an affair ended, as had that one, I always felt torn, but never guilty! I had convinced myself, that there was still plenty of magic in the air, and the nearness of Johnny merely confirmed my optimistic beliefs. I realised then, that I was head over heels in love and began to hope, that this night would never end.

To my surprise, Johnny suggested that I should rent a room from Irma, for which he would be responsible financially. He explained that he would be stationed at Zeltweg for 2 to 3 months, and that this would give us an opportunity, to get to know one another. His fiery determination overwhelmed me completely, and made me agree to all his wishes. All my ambitions for my career, just vanished into thin air, and all that mattered was Johnny's love.

When the evening was over, Johnny accompanied me to Irma's house, where all three of us sat down and discussed the renting of her spare room, to which she happily agreed. Indeed, she was extremely pleased for both of us and said so.

The following day, I phoned my mother and told her that I would like to help Irma with her tailoring, and that I would like to stay on for a few weeks.

As my mother had known Irma and her entire family for many years, she was quite happy for me to stay on, but reminded me not to give up on my singing lessons, which I promised not to do.

The rest of the day, I spent walking around on cloud nine, in anticipation of Johnny's return at 6 p.m.

He arrived with two suitcases, which we both unpacked, looking at each other sheepishly like two children embarking on a forbidden adventure.

Johnny looked at the double bed, which was provocatively taking up most of the space in the room, and before I knew what was happening, we were both kissing and cuddling on it.

It was only Irma's firm knock on the door that reminded us that we were not alone. She told us to hurry up, in order to get our evening meal at the mess.

As food was the second most important thing in my life, I quickly jumped up, adjusted my dress, in readiness to go; but Johnny pulled me back onto the bed, saying: "I had something far better in mind."

To which I hurriedly replied, *"Von der Liebe allein kann Ich nicht leben!"* - - - - - "From love alone, I cannot survive!"

He burst into laughter and said: "I thought you were the romantic type?"

As if on cue, my stomach started to rumble, and this luckily convinced Johnny, that there was nothing else for it, but food would have to come first.

We joined Irma and Ralph at the mess hall, where we dined and danced the night away. I was so deliriously happy that I could have danced till dawn.

On the way home, my mind sobered up, and I realised that I was entering a serious love affair, mildly afraid of the consequences. Up until now, I had never had a physical relationship with a man, and I was sure that Johnny had no idea that I was still a virgin. Yet, I was prepared to dismiss all fears and doubts, for the love of this man.

When we got home Johnny asked me, why I suddenly seemed so apprehensive, whilst he was beginning to caress and kiss me, undoing the small buttons on the front of my dress. Although I did not understand all that he said, it was the way he expressed his love and the hopes he shared for our future life together, that convinced me to surrender myself, to his tender loving care.

To my surprise he removed every part of my clothing, laying it carefully over a chair saying: "I want to gaze at you, as God created you." And as I lay naked across the bed, he undressed himself, giving me the opportunity to survey his perfectly proportioned figure. His bronzed torso, created a sharp contrast, to his blond wavy hair.

Nervously, I tried to engage him in small talk, but he bent over me, nestling my body beneath his and said: "Hush now darling, there is only one thing that I want to say to you. Love is supreme, it's either all or nothing, and you are everything to me. I love you."

The physical attraction between us was so strong, that any further dialogue became unnecessary, as I floated into seventh heaven.

As the days went by, Johnny was not only the great lover, but also a great, but strict teacher, instructing me in the correct use of the English language. Often, I had to repeat phrases over and over again, just like Eliza Doolittle; and each day, he reminded me more and more of Professor Higgins. He even resorted to blackmail, threatening to withold my favourite cakes, until I read my given sentences correctly.

Between the nights of passion, and his strict behaviour during our 'lessons', it sometimes felt as if I was living with two distinctly separate men. But I never lost an opportunity for mischief, so it was no wonder that he became stricter and stricter.

Once I put a pair of empty spectacle frames on him, which definitely made him resemble Professor Higgins. When he saw himself in the mirror, determined not to be distracted, he could not help but laugh at his own reflection, thus bringing that particular lesson to an end.

Of course it did not take me long to divert his attention, to the more passionate side of our relationship, to which he remarked: "And then you wonder why I am so strict with you? You are always thinking up ways and means, of diverting my attention. If you keep this up you will never learn any English; whatever am I going to do with you?"

As the weeks passed so quickly, we both became anxious that time was running out on us, as we wanted to behold every moment we spent together. Johnny, even covered up the clocks over the weekends, so that we could live timeless.

During one of these weekends, we attended a village dance. By accident, Johnny spilled some red wine on his best jacket and we left early to correct the damage. He gave me the jacket, which I took into the kitchen to clean. As I had to immerse the jacket in water to soak the stain, I checked the pockets to remove anything he might have in them. He had left his wallet in the outside pocket which I laid on the kitchen-table. But to my utter surprise I found two letters which had only recently been stamped, in his inside pocket. As he had not mentioned the receipt of any correspondence, I became curious! The envelopes were open, so I took out their content and stared aghast at the tender opening lines which I read: 'My Darling Johnny, I can hardly wait for your homecoming. The baby and I miss you terribly. As you can see from the enclosed photo, he has grown a lot, since you last saw him . . . .'

I did not need to read any further, and with tears in my eyes, I examined the photo of the blonde, pretty, young woman and her child. I felt betrayed and made up my mind, not to say anything of my sad discovery, in the hope that Johnny would have the decency and courage to tell me himself. I put the letters back into the pockets and busied myself with the removing of the stain.

I must have been a fairly long time in the kitchen as Johnny came in, started kissing the nape of my neck and said: "Gosh you're gonna wash the fibre away, if you keep at it for much longer." I was drained of emotion, and as he turned me around, he beheld a shocked and lifeless face. Concerned and startled, he immediately suggested that I should lie down. I was still hoping that he would tell me, but when he joined me in bed, there was no sign of him wanting to talk to me, so I evaded any further contact with him, by saying that I was unwell and just needed some sleep. Johnny would not let the matter rest there and said, that there must be something else and he kept on probing, until I finally reminded him, that he would have to go back to England fairly soon, and that this had added to my misery.

The following morning to my horror, he suggested desertion from the Royal Air Force, assuming another name and moving to Switzerland. He also assured me, that he would be able to get a job quite easily there, with a civil airline.

I couldn't believe my ears, I still longingly waited for some statement about the girl in England, but none was forthcoming. Instead, he was making even more outrageous plans of shedding every last ounce of responsibility left. But I still did not say anything, but reminded him of his oath of allegiance that he took to become an officer, and told him that I would never marry a deserter. He replied that this was the last answer he had expected from me, as to him all that mattered was the love we shared.

He had left me no option but to confront him with the facts. "What about your girl and child in England?" I asked, with a calmness that surprised even my own ears.

His face went bright red, he clenched his fists and said: "You were spying on me and reading my mail, how dare you?"

Suddenly before me, stood the other Johnny Spitfire, the man who was prepared to play a double game, regardless of the hurt he was inflicting on all of us. He pulled himself together, when he realised that this type of attack, was really no defence for what he had done. He then had the cheek, of all things, to propose an amicable arrangement.

My patience had been tried beyond its limits. As he had also abused my trust, I retorted angrily: "What are you suggesting? One weekend a month perhaps with me, and one with your girl-friend and child in England?''

"Don't be so flippant, you have no conception of how much I really love you," he replied, and tears began to stream down his face.

My anger melted, I found it impossible to me mad with someone, woman, man or child, when the floodgates opened. So, to comfort him, I put my arms around him and told him that he was not to upset himself any further, ... between us, we would find a solution.

This was the first occasion, in our entire time together, that my feet were actually firmly on the ground, as during our torrid love affair I had floated in a land of make-belief, where the possibility of pregnancy, seemed unreal. But now for the first time, the frightening thought that on top of everything else I might also be pregnant hit me straight in the stomach, and I began to feel sick. A picture of my life in ruins, with the possibility of a small child, which would now be born outside a loving relationship. The thought of having to bring it up on my own, was sufficient to make me realise that the gravity of the situation I found myself in, would make my life on earth a living hell.

Johnny, who had by now abandoned his plans of desertion, went on duty as usual and left me to ponder over the future.

I spent the rest of the day, trying to sort out my priorities. By the end of of the day, the only decision I had reached was that I wanted to go back home, to the protective warmth of my mother's arms.

To my surprise, Johnny returned home on a motor bike. When I told him that I wished to see my mother, he immediately suggested that we used the motor bike, to visit her.

I changed into trousers, a warm sweater and a scarf, and off we went. The roads were full with heavy military transport and should have slowed us down considerably, but Johnny did not reduce his speed, but kept weaving in and out of the lorries, with the drivers waving their fists at him, for his daring. Johnny shouted to me to hold him tighter, as he increased the speed even more and began racing the bike through the centre of the traffic. It was then, that I realised, that he was trying to put an end to both our lives.

I panicked, and started to scream at him, to slow down. When this had no effect, I pleaded with him and even took one of my arms from around his waist, hitting him hard on the back of his flying jacket, in an attempt to bring him back to reality. I was convinced that in his mind, Johnny was in his Spitfire, and that the enemy had become the transport.

A large lorry on the opposite side of the road flashed his

headlights, blinding us. It was this lorry driver that had saved our lives, as the blinding flash of light, brought Johnny back down to earth, and to his senses. He slowed the bike down and pulled into the side of the road.

The lorry driver behind us stopped too, got out and called him "A bloody fool" adding: "If you want to kill yourself, that is your business, but you have no right to kill the rest of us, too. Didn't you realise that this is an ammunition transporter; you could have blown us all to kingdom come, you idiot."

Johnny apologised and after a further lecture on road safety, the driver got back into his lorry, and drove off.

We sat on the side of the road for at least fifteen minutes, like two lost souls. Finally Johnny apologised to me, and urged that we should continue our journey, saying: "I really don't know what got into me. I promise, I usually ride very carefully." We got back onto the bike and continued the rest of the trip in silence, and at a slower speed.

My mother was very surprised at our subdued behaviour, and remarked how ill I looked. I assured her that it was just the ride that had taken the wind out of my sails, and that I would be all right after a nice cup of tea.

Whilst we were sipping our tea, I told my mother that Johnny had been posted back to England and that I would soon be returning home. When we had finished our tea, mother insisted that we stayed for something to eat and ushered us into the living-room, whilst she went into the kitchen, to prepare a meal.

When we were alone, Johnny finally began to talk about his past, explaining his involvement with the English girl and her child. He told me that they were neighbours, who had indulged in a brief wartime affair of which the boy, was a result. But he assured me that he never really loved her, not the way we had loved one another. I wanted so much to believe him, but the hurt ran too deeply. However, I could not erase my memory of the happy times we had shared at Zeltweg.

As the evening progressed, the big black cloud that had been hanging over us disappeared. Johnny asked me to play the piano and our favourite melody, which I had sang to him often. '*Ich weis es wird einmal ein Wunder geschehen und da werden 1000 Maerchen wahr, so schnell kann doch keine Liebe vergehen die so gross war und so wunderbar.*' 'I know that sometime, a miracle will happen . . . where 1,000 fairy-tales will come true, ... no love can disappear so quickly, ... that once was so great and so wonderful.'

We sang this together, thus cementing on the surface, the rift that had opened up between us.

As the evening drew to a close and I lowered the lid of the piano, Johnny suddenly put his hand over mine, as if helping me to shut it. This gesture took me right back to the day we met, when then he had placed his hand over mine, to help me shut the door. Only then, it was the beginning of a new chapter in our lives, and it seemed sad that now, it was closing, in the same way it had begun, and I couldn't help, but cry.

"Please don't darling," Johnny said, and tried to kiss me, but I moved to evade any further physical contact, as the hurt was already too much to bear.

I moved towards the corner of the room, which had a 'Madonna and Child' with a Bible by its side standing on a pedestal. Johnny rushed over to me, picked up the Bible, pulled me back into the centre of the room, by the coffee-table and made me sit down, with him in front of it. He then took my hand, placed it underneath his hand on top of the holy book and said in dead earnest: "Will you swear to me, that IF you are pregnant, you will contact me?" Without allowing me to answer, he continued: "I promise, that wherever I am, even if I end up in Timbuctue I shall come at once to marry you. Will you swear on the Bible?"

Johnny had no idea what those few words had done to me. He had, without knowing it, shut the lid on the coffin of our relationship, thus burying a love, where I had given my all, where I had been prepared to give up the possibility of a brilliant stage career, just for him. The deepest hurt was the tiny word 'IF'. I decided then and there, that no matter what the future held, even if I were pregnant, Johnny would never know about it. Having been brought up as a Catholic, abortion would be out of the question, and I would bring the child up alone, telling it one day, when it was old enough, that his father was dead. As Johnny had destroyed my trust and belief in him, by telling me so often that our love was the most important thing in his life, now suddenly qualifying it with an 'IF', I saw no reason to be truthful with him, and swore on the Bible that I would keep him informed.

We stayed overnight at my mother's, and returned to Zeltweg the next morning, pretending that all was well.

However, when we arrived back at Irma's, we agreed that Johnny should from now on stay at his RAF quarters, until it was time for him to leave for England.

I stayed on with Irma for a few days, but felt thoroughly miserable, with Irma remarking that I had become impossible to live with. Yet, I could not open my heart to her, and decided that the time had come to go back home.

A few days later, Ralph phoned me from the mess to let me know, that he and Johnny would be leaving for England in a couple of days.

Forewarned, was forearmed, as far as I was concerned. So I confided in my mother about Johnny, the girl and their baby in England. She was deeply upset, but relieved that I had finally come to my senses, adding that she hoped that this had taught me a lesson, and that from now on I would put my career above everything. I promised faithfully to do so, at the same time enlisting my mother's help, should Johnny try to come to say goodbye.

As expected, he arrived on the second day, to say his farewells.

My mother was well prepared, and informed him that I had left for Vienna and would not be back for some days. She pretended to be sorry that he had missed me, and explained if only he had phoned . . . . . how things might have been different. Alas, I had locked myself into my bedroom and heard every word that was said.

Johnny had sounded agitated, even angry when he asked: "Why, for God's sake? Why did she suddenly have to go to Vienna?"

But my mother did not weaken and kindly replied: "Well young man, time stands still for no-one. She received an invitation for an audition after all this time, and rushed off. You know yourself, how rare these opportunities are and that no time must be lost in taking them up, so I myself urged her to take the night train, which she did."

My mother's calm and kindly manner had convinced him as he finally bid her farewell saying: "She is a lovely girl your daughter, I wonder if I might have a photo, so that I shall never forget her."

My mother removed the photo from the wall, that was hanging there of me, and gave it to him.

As she opened the front door for him, I walked over to the window, to take one last look at him. It was raining heavily outside, as I watched his motor cycle roar off, into the distance. I couldn't help but wonder whether it was merely coincidence, that we should part on a similar kind of day, as the one that we had met on. That had also been a stormy, rainy day, which now reflected my inner feelings precisely. Johnny Spitfire Richards, had gone without breaking his word of honour, to the girl waiting back home in his native England. But I knew that every time I would see a plane soaring high above in the skies, he would return to haunt me, in the recesses of my heart. Why? Oh why was it so hard to forget?

The weeks had passed uneventfully, and November had arrived with even more troops to occupy the Steiermark. The British armed forces commandeered every available room as billets, and we too, that was my mother and I had two NCOs placed into what had been my spare sitting-room. I took little notice as I had more important things on my mind. All my energy was now directed towards getting an engagement as a singer.

As the Nazis had already robbed me of seven years of my life, I now felt that there was no time to lose.

Glancing through our local newspaper I read: 'Talented, attractive girls wanted for the stage. Apply to the Manager, Captain P. Elliott, Leoben Theatre!'

I made an appointment by telephone and was told to come the following Monday at 10.30 a.m.

Some twenty girls were already there, and a friendly looking British soldier told me to line up over there at the end of a mile long queue, saying: "You never know your luck miss." As I stood at the end of the long, dimly lit corridor, I could hear dancing and singing echoing around the walls with periodic floods of girls dressed in various attire, bustling through the already crowded corridor. I was most impressed by the stage costumes swishing past me like butterflies, but more so by the distinctly pretty looking girls that wore them.

As I was standing there, I became more self-conscious by the minute and eventually could actually feel my stocking slipping. Discreetly or so I believed, I lifted my skirt to adjust it.

Suddenly, a man appeared behind me, out of nowhere, saying: "Your talents would definitely be wasted in the chorus."

"Oh you think so do you?" I smartly replied, and turned my back on him in a haughty manner, thinking that this would make it perfectly clear what I thought of peeping Toms.

But he was not in the least perturbed as he continued: "I am the manager Captain Elliot."

Blazing at the audacity of the man, I snapped back at him sarcastically: "Oh I do beg your pardon, I am the Countess Maritza, I must admit that I did not expect to meet such illustrious company backstage."

That startled him and for a moment he seemed unsure of what to say, but nevertheless replied in a firm voice: "What spirit . . . . and what an actress I could make of you . . . . . follow me."

As he walked past me in an authoritative manner, I realised that I had been speaking to the genuine article. My instincts told me to go back home, especially after I had just made such an exhibition of myself, but home was poor and desolate, and my only chance was here in the theatre to make a future for myself, so I swallowed my pride and followed him into his office.

He seemed a little more subdued when we got into his office and gave me some lines to read, but I noticed that he was scrutinising me closely. When I had finished he said: "Your English needs a good deal of polishing, so I will tell you what I shall do, I will take you in hand personally. You are to look upon me as a friend, as a good working relationship is of the utmost importance."

"Nothing else?" I asked to unnerve this rock of self-importance and self-assuredness.

"No, not for the moment, unless you can sing?" he replied.

He had chosen to ignore the pointedness with which my question had referred to his term 'friend and good working relationship'. So there was nothing else for it, I gave up and demurely replied: "If you have a piano, I shall sing for you."

"Follow me," was his smart reply as he made his way to another door in the room, which opened to an even bigger room with a grand piano in full view.

By the time I got into the room, Captain Elliott was already seated at the piano and enquired after my choice of song. I requested 'MAYTIME' to which he immediately played the introduction.

As I sang, his expression visibly relaxed and he exclaimed: "Wonderful, you have a very rich voice, really too good for the light stuff."

I stopped and enquired what he meant by 'stuff' adding "That's an ugly word Herr Captain."

He laughed freely now, and the ice was broken as he said: "Your English definitely needs some polishing." He then asked me to continue singing.

When I had finished, sincerely impressed, he praised my voice, deportment and looks and declared that he would take me on tour to Klagenfurt, where most of the British troops were stationed, after arriving from the Italian front.

Astonished I asked when and he replied: "Next week, so you had better get ready, and don't worry, we will supply you with all the clothes you will need for your performances."

Rather anxious, I protested that I had not rehearsed enough, but he assured me that this need not concern me now, as all of that would be done in Klagenfurt. As requested, I gave him my home address and telephone number for further instructions.

One week later, I was, as promised on a train to Klagenfurt, accompanied by Captain Elliott, who was sizing me up like a race-horse about to be entered for the 'Grand National'.

"To promote you," he said "I have to study you inside out. You do understand?"

I did of course understand, only my trust in men, had not exactly proved justified, over the past and that was what I told him.

"What a pity," was his only reply, as he now directed his attention to the window and began to survey the beautiful scenery we were travelling through. This gave me a short interval to study him and I noted that actually, he had an interesting face, with grey-blue eyes. Most of all it was his fascinating voice, that revealed far more than a face ever could, and I presumed he was a cultured man with tastes for the finer things in life.

After a while he turned his attention back to me and started discussing my debut saying, "When you walk onto the stage, I want you to mesmerize the men, not by taking your clothes off, but with your singing."

With that firmly in my mind, we arrived at our destination. After he had made arrangements for rehearsals and my further English lessons, he instructed his driver to take me to my aunt's house where I was to stay for two weeks, with strict instructions for an early night, as we had to begin bright and early the next day.

Although, I had not seen my relatives for a very long time, they were extremely pleased to have me staying with them, especially as through this temporary British connection, I had access to food, which as everywhere in Austria was still only available on the black market, and at an inflated premium.

As arranged, the car came to pick me up on the first day, so that I would have no difficulties in finding the place hereafter. The rehearsals were held in the town hall and I was excited at the prospect of this longed-for chance to sing. After some discussions, it was finally agreed that I should sing two numbers, one called 'Sweetheart' and the other called 'Jealousy'. The rehearsals for the first number went without flaw, but the second song presented me with some difficulty, as I could not help but laugh at the lyrics.

Captain Elliott eventually stopped playing for me, and asked whatever was the matter? So I told him that I could not for the life of me understand, why anyone would want to hear a song about 'blinds', for that was what the French called them. The captain looked at me, and when he realised the seriousness with which I had explained the matter and that I truly believed in what I was saying, he too started laughing uncontrollably. Somehow, I

G

realised that he was not laughing at the same thing that I was, and I became deadly serious asking him what he found so funny?

The joke was of course on me! He took out his dictionary and showed me what jealousy meant in English and then in German, "Eifersucht", of course. I felt terrible about my own stupidity, but Captain Elliott could only remark: "The sooner you start those English lessons, the better."

The night of my performance came, and with it the nerves that accompany a first time on the stage. To add to this was the discomfort of the dress I was wearing, which as it had been too big for me, was held in place by pins, which pricked me everytime I moved. But when the curtains went up, I sang as if my life depended on it. The audience was full of soldiers, and when I finished my songs, they flung their caps in the air and shouted for more, thus I repeated the refrain from 'Jealousy' twice, and it was only the fact that Captain Elliott rescued me by introducing the third act which stopped my having to stand and sing in that awful dress all night.

The third act was one of the finest violinists of the time, but I could still hear them in the dressing-room as I was changing, "We want the girl".

At that point Captain Elliott came into my dressing-room and said: "You see, you have made a great impact. You must come to Vienna."

I agreed, and told him that first of all though, I needed a pass from the Russians to let me over the border at Semering, as I had no intention to join the 'poor fools' who had tried unsuccessfully to cross without a pass and had wound up cutting wood for the Russian troops, or worse still, had ended up having to clean their quarters.

I returned home to St. Stefan, elated with my success and in the happy knowledge that Captain Elliott was going to obtain a work permit for me, so that I could perform in Vienna for the troops' entertainment, called ENSA.

To my complete surprise my mother announced that she had heard me sing at Klagenfurt on the British Forces Network channel on the radio. Needless to say, I had no idea that the show had been recorded for broadcasting but after my mother pronounced how good I was it nourished my ambition even more so to get to Vienna. How ironic life can be, Austria liberated, but still we were not free to move about in our own land, without the permission of our Liberators.

For the next few weeks, all I could think about was my singing career and my work permit.

As there was no sign in the post of my promised papers from Captain Elliott, I decided that I would have to take matters in my own hands. I had, quite by accident, found out from our local mayor, that Karl Steiner was now head of the Communist Party Headquarters in Vienna. This news had no sooner reached my ears, than I put pen to paper. I wrote of my plight explaining the circumstances in some detail appealing to his past feelings for me.

As there was no reply after seven days, I was ready to give up. But my mother told me not to be so impatient and asked me to think of another way. Why had I not thought of asking our lodgers for help, after all, they were British and might be able to?

The reason, this had not really occurred to me in my quest, was that I really did not have very much to do with either of them. In fact, I hardly ever had any contact, and what I had heard did not exactly endear them to me. The one was a Corporal Harold J. Ell, who seemed to be far too preoccupied with his drinking parties for me to make a friend of him; and the other was a burly Scot, by the name of Angus McDonald, and by all accounts a bit of a Romeo, with the ladies. So it was no wonder that I could hardly enlist their help.

One late afternoon, after a day out I came home to find my room door locked, and I could hear noises, soft music from my radio and occasional giggles emanate from inside, and I demanded that the door be opened, by whoever was in my room.

The strong Scottish accent of McDonald could be heard, shouting through the door: "Get lost you silly bitch."

Anger beyond belief welled up inside of me. I shouted back that I would fetch his commanding officer and went off to do so.

As I got to the British Headquarters which was the local gasthaus, I was told by the owner, that the C.O. was out for a stroll with his daughter Resi. I was livid, and stormed back home but this time twice as determined to get into my room.

The curtains were drawn, and the radio was still playing so I banged on the window and shouted, that I would smash it in if they did not open the door by the time I walked round there. To my surprise, this last threat, did the trick.

When I got to my room door, Mitzi, Dr Krempel's servant stood in the half-opened doorway in her undergarments and tried to calm me down. I was aghast at the shameless way, she was just standing there, and shouted at her: "What do you think my flat is? How dare you use it like a bordello?"

Her boy-friend came to the door half dressed, and told me to come in rather than make such a racket in the hallway.

I was disgusted and told them so, because McDonald was a married man with two boys. The photograph of his family stood by his bedside table. How dare he take this girl to my bedroom and moreover to my bed. I was no angel, but I always distinguished between love and lust, and certainly never in someone else's bed; and I pointed out to them that there was a time and place for everything. Both parties got the message and left.

At first I felt like fumigating the whole room. I hastily opened the windows and started stripping the bedclothes like someone demented. As if my radar antenna had suddenly been switched to full beam, I suddenly became aware that I was not alone.

As I turned to home in on this signal, there in the doorway, like a mirage in the desert, stood an impeccably dressed vision of Steiner, as large as life. He was really the last person on earth I had expected to see.

We greeted each other warmly and he asked: "Whatever happened? This place looks as if a bomb has hit it."

I hurriedly removed some of the bedding from the divan and bade him to take a seat.

He still smiled and remarked: "You're sure it's safe, you haven't got any explosives under here?"

It dawned on me now, that the battle was over, and I began to see things in a different light, much to the amusement of Steiner. I then explained in detail, what I had found on my return.

Karl listened to my ravings about the British soldier's behaviour. He then reminded me that this was merely a replay of my earlier experiences with the Russians, and that he was glad to see that my determination to rid the world of all the little Hitlers in it, had obviously not waned, adding: "Burgi, sometimes I think that you live in a world completely of your own making, where you would like for everything to fall into a neat little pattern of your choosing. Don't you realise that human nature is the same everywhere, and that it cannot be arranged to suit?"

"A fine statement coming from a communist, who want all people to be equal, yet live in a society where some are more equal that others, truly remarkable," I countered.

As I was making my point with forceful gestures gesticulating with my arms, Steiner pulled me into his arms, and kissed me into silence. When he released me from his embrace he said: "Please calm down, I did not come here to fight with you."

I smiled, as he gently placed his arms around me, his dark eyes still exuding a magnetic force, that suddenly made the past seem stronger than the present. How I wished that I had been stronger, regardless of his incapacity for physical love, in holding on to his love, which could have been far more rewarding than the physical passion of my last affair.

Just like in the old days, Steiner, as if guessing my thoughts said: "My desire for you has never ceased, but because I am harmless, you may toy with my feelings."

What a sad epitaph to what might have been. I gave him a big hug, and offered to make him tea, just like the English make it. He smiled and accepted. He followed me into the kitchen, where I diverted the conversation to my present predicament of the work permit, or more to the point, the lack of it.

He asked, what my reasons were, for so desperately wanting to be in Vienna, and teasingly said: "If there is a man behind this, you realise that I will not lift one finger to help you."

This made me smile too! So I reassured him that this time, my intentions were strictly 'professional', as I was determined to carve a name for myself, in the singing and acting world.

Karl pointed out that there was one big obstacle and said: "I really do wish that I could actually do something to get you there, but that is unfortunately beyond my powers, because your name is on a wanted list, of the Russians. You know of course why? No-one, not even you Burgi, can make a fool of a Russian general, and get away with it."

"Well, what did he expect me to do?" I retorted. "Tramp all over Eastern Europe as his mistress with him?"

Steiner lowered his eyes to avoid mine.

"Well?" I demanded. I suddenly realised that my temper was again getting the better of me, so I said in a much softer voice: "I am sorry, I didn't mean to snap at you, it's just that everytime I think about it, I get mad. Anyhow, let's change the subject, tell me what happened to you, when you went back to Sacha? I couldn't believe my ears when the mayor told us the other afternoon, that you are now at the headquarters in Vienna."

Steiner looked bemused, as he then explained all, saying: "I returned quite prepared to take any punishment, as you will probably remember, I was full of self-pity. So I went straight to the general and explained to him everything that had happened between us that afternoon, and that I had helped you get away. I also added that he could do with me as he pleased, as I was beyond caring . . . . . There was one moment, when I truly believed that he would do something drastic, and that was when he reached for his revolver, but to my amazement, he put his left hand on my shoulder, and told me that I had sacrificed enough without further punishment from him, and he ordered me to 'get out of his sight'. It was at that moment that I knew, that the bond of friendship between Sacha and I was broken forever. That was all really, he then had me posted to Vienna ahead of him, where I am still today, as the secretary of the Communist Party. But Burgi, let me add one more thing, whatever you may think of him, believe me when I tell you, that Sacha, after you left, was never the same man, and I firmly believe, even today, that he was passionately in love with you.''

''What, like Attila the Hun?'' I replied, and we both laughed.

However Steiner's face was deadly serious when he warned me, saying: ''Don't be too bold, take my advice and stay clear of Vienna, until the Russians have gone.''

But I swiftly replied: ''I can't wait that long, if I waited until then, I would probably be old enough to play 'The Merry Widow'!''

Karl did not seem to think this funny, as he persisted: ''Don't be so flippant, just to exist in Vienna is a giant struggle, least of all without a ration book, which you of course could not apply for because of Sacha, even if you did manage to get there.''

Karl Steiner left on the evening express train for Vienna, whilst I brooded over ways and means, of getting there.

Two months had elapsed and my high hopes of receiving a work permit by post from Captain Elliott had dwindled by the day, as Christmas 1945 was approaching!

In those days, the victors were our only salvation, and many a girl sold herself for a loaf of bread or less. Sex, without love, to me was abhorrent, and so I had devised a plan of my own, how to survive, without going to bed with any man. I was born with an ability to tease and tantalise, and I had acquired a cunning over the years, that made men feel protective towards me, which enabled me to keep them dangling on a string. Not a very nice character trait under normal circumstances, I agree, but at the time, I had little choice, survival was the keyword! And so it was, in this instance, as fate came to my aid once more, in the form of an 8th Army Corporal by the name of Harold James Ell.

He was a nice chap, nicknamed by his pals 'Errol Flynn', because of his striking resemblance to the star of the big screen, especially when he smiled. Ell, as I called him, was in a privileged position, driving Brigadier Templer around. A perk of his job, was the use of the Humber staff car, when the brigadier had no need of it. Although, it wasn't strictly allowed, Ell took me for drives in this luxurious car, which made me the envy of many a girl in the district. Yet, he had only eyes for me, and even shared his own food ration with my mother and I.

The British troops had settled quite well into village life and made every effort to become part of the community, by organising all kinds of events which would bring them into contact with the locals and promote a relationship of peaceful cohabitation. My favourite, were the dances that were advertised.

Martina, my best friend and I, always waited eagerly for the new posters to go up. We had to laugh about the advertisement, which read: 'Dance, on Saturday Night, with Free Sandwiches and Tea.' Whatever would we do next, to fill our hungry stomachs?

It immediately brought to mind a song from the 30s, which originated, when a good-looking young man fell on hard times and had to dance for a dime, to make his living! So, always at the ready with some light relief, I danced in the empty baker's shop for Martina, singing: "*Armer Gigolo, du must tanzen . . . .*".

This had Martina in stitches as she begged me to stop, reminding me, that really we shouldn't laugh, because now it was our turn, going to a dance for some tea, and sandwiches.

Ell took me to this dance, but Martina's words were still ringing in my ears and took the enjoyment away, as I began to feel undignified.

From that moment on, I knew that I had to think hard, of another way to leave here. It was no good waiting for a future to come to me! I would have to shake myself out of the complacency, that had overcome my whole thinking now and work, at making my future happen. So when Ell mentioned that he would not be seeing me for a few days, because he had been put in charge of transport, delivering and collecting lorries from Udini in Italy, which were destined for Vienna; my ears stood to attention!

At every opportunity thereafter, I described longingly to Ell how wonderful life would be, if I could go to Vienna. Of course I never mentioned, that I did not have a pass or a working permit, so he naturally just assumed, that I could not go there by train, because of lack of money.

Some weeks went by, and I was surprised that Ell still wanted to date me, as my continual 'talk' about Vienna, made even my own ears shudder. Yet, he never complained, but listened patiently.

But one morning, I was rewarded for my hard work, I had just opened my bedroom window, as a British convoy was passing, when the whole entourage stopped and one lorry turned, and came up our drive. Ell jumped out and raced up the steps inside the house, shouting: "If you really want to go to Vienna, now is your chance, but you have to be quick, I cannot hold my men up for more than five minutes."

For one moment I thought, I was dreaming, but my mother's voice soon returned me to the moment at hand, as she urged me to hurry. I grabbed a bag, stuffed in my pyjamas and went in what I stood, my riding trousers, a thick sweater, a jacket and a warm woollen cap. With tears streaming down her face, my mother hurriedly kissed me goodbye, wished me luck and told me to go, and so we set off!

Once inside the cabin of the five-ton lorry, Ell flung a blanket over my shivering legs and introduced me to his driver, who by all accounts was a good friend of his, and who appeared to approve of me whole-heartedly. I had no fear of Ell, as he was really the most harmless of all my so-called 'boy-friends', as he was by far too soft with someone like me, who could just twist him around my little finger. I also knew that when it came to the crunch, he would be just the person to protect me.

Almost certain in this knowledge, I asked Ell what his load was. "Thousands of yards of wire, rolled together" was his innocent reply!

My mind immediately saw this as the ideal solution. I would crawl inside the wire, and thus hide until we were over the Semering border.

So far so good, but what about Ell, echoed my mind. 'You haven't even explained to him that you are a wanted person, and that you have no pass or work permit! Don't worry, something will turn up' I told myself, and something did! The Russian border!

It could be seen quite clearly in the distance, but Ell explained that it was at least two miles away yet, and stopped the convoy for a rest, so that the drivers could have their tea and sandwiches, before crossing. Ell shared his ration of food with me, and we all got out to sit by the roadside to eat. The other drivers had come to join us, probably more out of curiosity, than anything else, as civilians were a rarity on their trips, and were, as a general rule not allowed to travel on military transport. But Ell had explained during the journey that the rules had occasionally been bent, and that as long as the passengers' papers had been in order, the border guards usually let them through without any fuss.

When he had finished his tea, he suddenly turned and said: "That reminds me, you had better give me your papers now!"

Nervously, I rummaged through my bag, pretending that I could not find them. But this bluff did not go down well, as he pulled me to my feet and shouted: "How dare you?"

The game was up and I could see that any excuses would cut no ice with him, so I used the only weapon left to a woman in my situation. Tears began streaming down my face, as I stood there, half my bread still in one hand, clutching my bag with the other, looking totally lost and helpless. The other drivers too joined in, all talking at once, saying how dangerous it was to try and fool the Russians. "They will arrest us all," one driver shouted, this made me cry even more.

Seeing how distressed I was, being shouted at by all the drivers, Ell then took charge of this awful situation, suddenly shouting louder, than anyone else: "I am in command of this bloody transport, and I am not abandoning this poor girl, here on the roadside . . . . . I may only be a small man, but so was Monty . . . . and he out-foxed Rommel."

At that moment my inner belief in him was rewarded, he was truly my hero, and my defender, a man who had risen above the limitations of his rank, and proved that he was a taller man, than all those who dwarfed him. I found no words with which to thank him, only the expression in my face, conveyed my deepest thanks.

There was no moment to lose now, as he bundled me into the back of his lorry, where I was confronted by huge bales of barbed wire. With the blanket over my back, I crawled into the centre of the furthest bale, and covered myself as best I could. Ell put the remaining bales on top, and to the side of the bale, where I was hiding in, and assured me that I was invisible.

As Ell shut up the back of the lorry, I thought: 'What a way to travel in my liberated Austria. Was this really what I had fought for?'

As the lorry drove off, I came to realise how uncomfortable my present mode of transport really was, as hundreds of little sharp pinpricks, made themselves apparent all over my body. However, I made no sound, determined to see this ordeal through, for which after all I had only myself to blame.

After a little while the lorry slowed down and finally came to a halt again. My heart pounded, as I heard the knock that we had arranged as a signal, to let me know, that we had reached the check-point. The guard's booming voice could be heard, enquiring what load they were carrying. To my horror, the guard then insisted on an inspection. I willed myself to remain calm, just as I had done in my Resistance days, when I had hidden myself under worse debris, than this, to stay alive. It all seemed somehow unreal, that now in supposed peace-time, I should have to resort to the same methods again, only this time to travel a few miles in a country that was supposed to be liberated.

As the guard stepped on the back of the lorry, my heart nearly missed a beat, as his weight bounced me around in this prickly cage, which now became painful, so I bit my lips to suppress my anguish.

After shining his torch into the back of the lorry, the guard jumped off and gave the all-clear to proceed.

Our lorry drove off and gained full speed, in next to no time. I was flung about in my 'cage', but the prickles from the barbed wire mattered little, now that I was on my way to Vienna.

After we were out of sight of the check-point, Ell stopped the convoy and helped me to extricate myself from my prison! I embraced him and thanked him to the applause of the other drivers, then I thanked each, and everyone for their help, as tears of joy were streaming down my face.

How could any of them really understand what it meant to be occupied, to have no freedom, but they all seemed pleased as they returned to their lorries.

"It's all over now, my girl," said Ell as he helped me back into the lorry, with a look in his eyes, that said more than the words he had just uttered.

I hoped I was mistaken, because all I wanted was friendship . . . . did he expect more? But I was too exhausted with the excitement of the past few hours and started to think of Vienna, the city renowned for its wine, women and song, but more so VIENNA the musical metropolis, the unforgettable melodies of Johann Strauss, Franz Schubert and Lehar, where Ludwig van-Beethoven spent the summer of 1817 and wrote his Ninth Symphony and men like Sigmund Freud, the father of psychoanalysis, was born. Perhaps destiny was just waiting for me to be discovered?

Vienna, City of My Dreams

As we drove along the nearly deserted streets, I was surprised at the sight of a very poorly dressed woman, pushing a handcart with a few belongings. This was not how I imagined it, the woman looked worse than the country people I had left behind. And I began to wonder in what sort of state I would find my own relatives, who lived in the 18th District, which as Ell informed me was now the American zone.

But before I could worry any further over the matter, we arrived. The house seemed undamaged and my dear aunt came outside to greet us, with Frau Fertsack, who was the old caretaker. As I introduced Corporal Ell to them, Frau Fertsack immediately curtsied, which somewhat astounded my companion, but of course this was understandable. After all, I had not told him that I was the niece of the Baroness von Haan. As the war years had made a nonsense of titles and the like, and as my mother had always been treated like the black sheep of the family, there seemed little point in mentioning such a connection.

I suppose, one look at my shabby appearance, would probably have made it difficult anyway, for anyone to believe that I had been brought up in a convent and that I belonged to a family which placed a high value on etiquette.

Ell, however, seemed to realise the difference of environment and quickly asked how to address my aunt. I told him as 'Frau Baronin', which he promptly did and excused himself, promising to call the following day with some food for us.

The word 'food', brought a smile to my aunt's face as we walked into the hall. We climbed up the familiar white marble staircase. Frau Fertsack following with my bag, and I asked what had happened to the lovely carpets that had once adorned it.

"Oh the Russians took them, Burgi," replied my aunt.

This did not surprise me as similar experiences had befallen our own village of St. Stefan. So I then related all my adventures over the past months to my aunt who listened avidly. We were soon joined by my two cousins, Mitzi and Nelly, who also listened eagerly like children listening to a fairy-tale, even though they were both considerably older than I.

As promised, Ell arrived the following evening, in the brigadier's car, which was filled with goodies. He had brought tins of corned beef, sardines, fresh bread and fruit and cigarettes. Nelly, who according to my aunt was a chain-smoker and impossible to live with when she had none, thought that Ell was 'Santa Claus'! Ell's gifts were very much appreciated by everyone, and my aunt bade him to have tea with us.

As we were sitting there in the splendid dining-room, which had been designed for the royal members of the Habsburg family, with its gold panelled walls and antique chandeliers which were glistening and enhancing the fine porcelain that we were eating from, I wished that we had some means of recording that moment for ever. It seemed that all had been turned upside-down. Generations of Haans had lived and died in this house since 1838, and entertained only the highest society, and here we were, glad of the company of a corporal, because he had brought us food.

Similar thoughts must have crossed my aunt's mind, as she remarked after Ell's departure: "Isn't it odd, how history always completes a full circle? The first powerful corporal was Napoleon, then came Hitler, and now it's Corporal Ell."

We continued to discuss our lives in general and came to the conclusion, that my singing career must have priority above all other matters, and that I should register at the academy as soon as possible.

Indeed, I did register, and arranged to meet a Professor Fischer the next day. He was a very distinguished-looking man, and I was glad, that my cousin Mitzi had come along to give me some moral support. I had worked myself up into a lather, so that when I was actually face to face with him, my voice just disappeared.

"That often happens," he said, "but you must learn to conquer your nerves young lady, as the theatre needs new and exciting talents, and who knows, you could be just what we've been looking for."

He sat down at the piano and started to play the introduction of Lehar's 'Vilja', indicating to me to begin . . . . and I did.

After I finished the song, he paused, and then exclaimed: "Not only have you got a wonderful voice, but a delivery second to none, that I have heard lately. We must practise, for practise makes perfect, and when you appear in front of your audience, they must of course say . . . . . ah, she was trained by Fischer.''

Mitzi was so glad that I had regained my voice, that she went a little over the top in congratulating me. I could see the professor smiling out of the corner of his eye, as we arranged for my lessons. Before we left, he gave me a list of dos and don'ts. This read as follows: Early to bed; Plenty of fresh air; No smoking, (thank heavens I never had started!); No heavy love affairs . . . . Now that was a tall order!

Even though the professor lived in the third district, which meant that we would have a really long way to walk home to the eighteenth district, I felt like dancing. With the prospect of a singing career in front of me, I could have climbed 'Mount Everest' in order, to get home. Mitzi kept glancing sideways at me to make sure, that my feet were still on the ground. They were, but my head was already way up in the clouds, as I saw myself appearing at the Volksoper, as a star, bewitching the audiences, partnering the dashing tenors, like Fred Liewehr, who was my favourite. I was full of ideas of how to present the best of me, imagining my public spellbound at my very appearance. And why not? After all I had been acting on Hitler's stage for seven years, to stay alive, and had survived. It was now my turn to become famous.

The professor's instructions, to stay clear of torrid love affairs, with only light flirtations permitted, was enough to ensure that we would have something to eat, as Corporal Ell, was more than eager to merely be in my company; so everything would work out alright. More than happy with this portrait of my future, I began to swing my handbag in the air as we walked along the Gentzgasse, which was now nearly by our home.

Suddenly, it was snatched off me by an American soldier driving past in a jeep. Mitzi shouted at him, but he laughed and waved to us. We gave chase, but the vehicle slowed down, only to rev up again, until finally it disappeared round a corner, where it vanished completely.

It was not the money I had, which mattered, but my aunt's ration books, which I was carrying. I was frantic when we reached my aunt's home.

She however urged that calm and reason were what was required and said: "You must report this gangsterous behaviour at once to the American headquarters, Burgi.''

My aunt insisted, and so off we set for the Cottage district, and Uncle Otto's villa which in fact had been comandeered as the headquarters for the Americans by General Mark Clark.

Before we could enter, we had to state our business, whereupon we were quickly ushered in to see a Captain Bass. He rose and was ultra polite, asking for a description of the soldier and detail of the stolen item. All we could remember between us was the jeep. So I explained that during that time of day, surely there could not have been that many, as one would assume that they reported when they left for duty and returned.

It made complete sense to the captain, who was angry as we were, and he promised not to leave a stone unturned to recover my stolen bag, assuring us that the guilty party would be punished. I left my address and could not help myself from mentioning, that the house we were now standing in actually belonged to Baron Otto von Haan, who was my uncle.

"That will speed him up Mitzi," I whispered as we left, much to the amusement of my cousin. We hurried home, to meet Ell who had promised to come by with some food, as this was far more important now than the wretched handbag, only to find that he had left a note with my aunt to say that he would be unable to come as he had to take the brigadier on an unexpected journey.

What a disaster, two losses in one day, with the latter leaving us with only two days of food left in the larder. There was no point in letting the present situation get on top of us, so we played bridge as usual, hoping for some small miracle.

Indeed we did not have to wait long. It appeared that very evening, in the person of Captain Bass. He arrived with a carton of cigarettes, oranges and my white handbag, which now contained three pairs of the most fabulous silk stockings. What could one say? . . . . . but, welcome . . . . to our home and please do call again. One did not stand on ceremony, probing into what was normal, but accepted gifts from the horse's mouth, with gratitude and charm. Captain Bass told us his life story during the evening, explaining that he originated from Michigan, USA. He was the son of a pastor, a fact, which impressed my aunt no end. I however, was not quite as easily taken in and immediately searched for a motive in his bringing my property back, personally.

My cousin Mitzi must have had a similar thought in her mind, as she whispered to me saying "He came to see you of course." (And why not, he was a respectable officer and gentleman)! Of course she was right, one more or less did not matter, so when he asked my aunt if he could take me to his American Club, I was not surprised that she gave him permission to do so.

In minutes I changed my dress and off we went to his waiting car, which was standing by the front door. It was then that I realised that all had already been arranged in advance. During the car ride he told me that his christian name was Wayne. From his manner and general behaviour, I have to admit that he was different from the other Yanks, I had seen running about. In fact he was rather gentle, a little intense and almost shy, as he explained to me how sad it was that the American Air Force had bombed historical towns like Vienna. I agreed with him and we had hardly noticed how quickly the time had passed, as the car pulled up in front of the American Club.

As we got out of the car, such an awful noisy row could be heard from inside, that we both decided to go for a drive to the Vienna Woods instead. It was there that Captain Bass suggested that we visit the elegant restaurant Huebner, which overlooked the city. It was obvious that money was no object, and I ordered the best. As we sat there in the comfortable chairs, overlooking Vienna, hundreds of lights glistened before our eyes, yet with the darkness, one could not see war damage, only the silhouettes of prominent buildings.

Slowly Wayne reached for my hand, caressing my wrists. His lips spelt out all the words I had heard so many times in the past, but somehow they sounded exciting, sensuous and flattering. What girl would not like being wooed and told that her eyes were beautiful, and that it was not just a wild infatuation, but the beginning of a love for all seasons. All I really wanted was a good meal and the company of an intelligent man with whom I could discuss my career. It was refreshing that I could do this with Captain Bass, who was rather in control of his feelings, and did not appear to want me only for the sexy role that other men wanted me to play. However, in the back of my mind I could feel that he was trying to rush me, and as the evening drew on, I had to make it very clear that I was only interested in a platonic relationship. He agreed and said "Just to hold you in my arms and dance with you, will make me happy honey."

We danced until midnight and arrived back on my doorstep at 1 a.m., where Wayne kissed me good-night and arranged to meet me again.

At breakfast my cousins pounced on me to tell them everything, in particular Mitzi, who was a romantic and still believed at the age of fifty, that there was such a thing as the perfect lover. I quickly had to assure her that even if there was such a thing, it certainly wasn't Wayne. My other cousin, the spirited Nelly then bombarded me with a barrage of questions, and I had to convince her too, that Bass was not the type of man who could send me into hysterics. This last comment made them all laugh.

January 1946.

My singing lessons continued twice a week, and I began to make great strides with songs from my favourite Opera 'Csarewitsch' by Lehar. *"Warum had jeder Frühling auch nur einen Mai . . warum bleibt Dir das dumme Herz nicht ewig treu . . warum hast Du mich so geküsst . . und so geliebt . . warum?"* — "Why has every Spring only one May . . and why did you have to love me so much . . why?"

Why indeed? Too many men had loved me, or so I believed, thus I could sing songs like these with feeling. Professor Fischer was entranced and delighted at my interpretation, and he said "If you sing as well as that on stage, you will have standing ovations." I believed what he told me and directed all my energy towards my career, studying my roles in depth to give the best possible performance. I often asked myself if it was possible to adopt a superficial attitude, with which one could fool one's friends and acquaintances and still be successful. By daylight it all made some sense, but at night when I was in my bed, I started thinking about those scintillating affairs and the rollocking episodes. These thoughts turned the lamb into the tigress.

Cold reality and ambition stood before me. It was now the week prior to my birthday on the 21st January, and Corporal Ell telephoned to say that he would gladly accept the invitation to my forthcoming birthday party. I was a little apprehensive, visualising the meeting of my two boy-friends, Captain Bass versus Corporal Ell.

When I mentioned this matter to my aunt, she was not amused and reminded me that I would have to stay on good terms with both of them, if we were to survive the present food shortage. Mitzi called them my two Cs, for captivating company, but I however pointed out that it was more likely that they stood for calculating company.

My birthday became a small social event, with twenty-three people all around my own age, with the exception of four British and one American guest. To the sheer delight of my relatives, they all got on gloriously, toasting me and their victory. The old saying that there is safety in numbers really paid off. Adding spice to this gathering, I did a spot of astrology and discussed the various birth signs, which caused great excitement, as everyone wished to know what life held in store for them.

Being an Aquarius lady, I pulled no punches, and declared that this was the sign of formal friendship, which perceived the world in an unusual way, spotting things that others might never notice. The guests cheered me on to tell them more, in particular about my love life. I found this to be a somewhat impertinent question, but laughingly told them that my cool, calm image, was a disguise, in that I preferred my boy-friends to sprint, rather than to run the marathon. I was glad when the questions finally stopped, and the evening's entertainment diverted to dancing and singing, leaving everyone with a happy smile. By this time I was too tired, to really examine all my presents, most of which were expensive imported flowers. We had to open the windows, as the smoke together with the exotic scents from my flowers created an atmosphere not unlike that of an opium den. My cousin Nelly, who smoked like a chimney, and who was also a little bit tipsy into the bargain, seemed the most affected. We had to put her into the bath to sober her up, leaving the shower running cold over her head. In a way I felt sorry for her. She looked so helpless, bedraggled and wet, yet was still happily singing in English "Who stole my heart away . . who?" To look at her I thought who indeed would do such a thing to Nelly, who although approaching fifty, still gave the impression of a little girl.

Refreshed and bewildered over the impeccable behaviour of my two boy-friends, I began a new week with the eagerness to conquer all, and the will to turn myself into a new disciplined person. But alas, the mechanical life was not for me, I needed inspiration and love, even if only from my relatives. Consequently discipline came and went. My aunt and my dear cousins however, were only concerned about food and the material side of living, therefore finding it difficult to acquiesce to my needs of inspiration and love.

Professor Fischer had the remedy in hand. He organised a small concert at the Belvedere Palace, Prince Eugen's former residence. The performance was arranged for ten days' time. I immediately tossed aside, all that stood in my way and went into rehearsals with every ounce of my being. I was to sing a duet with Fred Liewehr, hailed as the best 'Danilo' in the business. Although he was nearly twenty years my senior, he was extremely handsome and visually created the picture of my perfect partner. Further, my repertoire included: "*Meine Lippen die küssen so heiss*" from Lehar's opera 'Guiditta', and I was to finish with "*Einer wird kommen . . . .* "

What more could I have possibly asked for? With all my favourite songs I threw myself into rehearsals like an angel possessed and found no time for anyone, not even Ell and Wayne. Yet, they never gave up and found comfort in talking to my cousins, who were thrilled to have company and the little bonuses that brought with it, like smokes, for my cousin Nelly, who really did find life difficult without them.

If luck was being handed out, I certainly must have been on the

H

end of receiving the lion's share, as I was being introduced to the foremost Musical Director, Peter Resch, who conducted the famous Salzburg Festival Orchestra and who was a composer in his own right. Not only was he brilliant, but also handsome. He immediately made a bee-line for me, which even though it was very flattering, did have its disadvantages, as his wife kept interrupting our rehearsals, by telephoning and then coming in person to watch from the French doors to ensure that nothing untowards was going on. This started Professor Fischer off, who also began watching me like a hawk. None of this would have mattered had something really been going on for them all to see. But to be stared at for no good reason really became unnerving, especially as all I wanted from Peter Resch was to learn to improve my own performance on the stage. I had no intention to make an impact behind the curtains, yet Resch could not divorce his professional assistance from his private feelings. It got to the point, where I dreaded going to rehearsals.

It was only my aunt who saved the day, by saying: "Well my dear, look at it like this, it's turning into an 'Opera Comique', before you even go on stage."

This quickly revived my sense of humour, and I paid little attention to anything going on around me from then on, concentrating only on my studies.

As the time for the concert drew closer, I got to know all the names of the VIPs that were to attend. This did not help a great deal, except that it's better the devil you do know, than the one that you don't. When I was told that Brissane, the most feared theatre critic was going to attend, I needed every ounce of my courage, not to falter in my aim. Yet, my family and friends encouraged me no end and with Fischer reminding me that I had the best musical director, so how could I possibly fail? Add to this, the woman with the magic fingers, and what had we got? A wardrobe that was increasing by the day, and one of which I could be proud of thanks to the nimble fingers of my seamstress, Frau Klima. She knew every inch of my body and every colour that suited me. She made it her motto to always enhance only the best asset, the rest, according to her would take care of itself. With me, she did not have too much of a problem as my measurements were 36 - 24 - 36. For the performance we chose three evening dresses, out of my impressive wardrobe. One was a tea rose, satin gown, cut to cling, which was adorned with a corsage of pink roses that were draped gracefully over the left shoulder. The second was made out of green chiffon, with yards of material pressed into tiny folds, falling like a waterfall from waist to floor, where they were trimmed with white marabou. The third was a tailored black velvet gown which had a very low back, and was held together by the tiniest straps.

The final dress rehearsal went well and Brissane's wife, who was a prima ballerina, came behind stage to have a look. She, although reserved in manner made it known that she thought that we had done well, a fact which somewhat lifted my ego to do even better, when I faced the audience.

16th February.

Indeed the concert was a big success. It rained flowers and applause with Professor Fischer leading Brissane himself on stage to greet me. But my greatest surprise came when the great critic in full view of the public knelt down before me, and on one knee exclaimed: "A new star is born, a new Luisa Katusch has arrived in Vienna."

Was it really possible that the greatest critic in our time had really thought I was so good? Lady Luck was truly smiling on me and I soon realised that he had no reason to tell anything but the truth as he saw it, the great Brissane certainly never wasted words of praise and would without a doubt, have cut me down, as he had done many of the greater artists than I, had I performed badly.

Now that my talent had been discovered, my career was assured. But still I felt uneasy, as glancing into the wings I found that there were far too many men all standing there waiting for me. I felt a little like a bird in an aviary, not quite sure what to do, when Professor Fischer came to the rescue, whisking me past the expectant faces to my dressing-room. There he told me to hurry and change as we had been invited to the Brissane's villa to meet, no less a person, than the great composer, Franz Lehar.

I changed in record time, though how I managed, I still don't know, as all the available space had been taken up with huge bouquets of flowers.

When the professor and I arrived at the villa, we were straightaway introduced to the great man himself, who with the most charming and disarming smile told me that he had been in the audience and had enjoyed my singing very much indeed. He also added that I was to check the card inside the roses he had sent to my dressing-room. Of course, with all the excitement, I had no time before arriving there, to even look at all the good wishes that had been accompanied by all the flowers, but I promised to do so as Lehar kissed my hand, and then went on to talk with some of the other guests.

Still in a spin, we continued to celebrate and songs from one of

Lehar's operas, from Paganini could be heard. Then came my turn, when Lehar demanded that I sing for him from 'Guiditta'. I was proud to oblige, and taking one rose, from a nearby vase, began waving it enticingly before the great composer and sang: "*Meine Lippen, die küssen so heiss . . . . meine Glieder, so schmiegsam und weiss . . . . in den Sternen da steht es geschrieben . . . . . du sollst küssen . . . . du sollst lieben.*"

What lyrics these were, but unfortunately they suffer in translation where they lose that sensuous and romantic quality which made even Lehar's eyes glisten with more than just appreciation of a good song. The night was still young, so we celebrated and drank only the best champagne and sang to our hearts' content.

And when I finally left, Lehar's voice was still ringing in my ears, "Don't forget to read my card Guiditta." It was well known that his roving eyes for beautiful women were never stronger than in the later years of his life. The moment he was introduced to me by Professor Fischer, I thought as he kissed my hand so very gently in front of the theatre audience, that I had landed on top of the heap, and that it would only be a matter of hours before he would ring me to invite me to his 'Rosen Schlossel'. The tension was nearly unbearable, yet in the past, such as it was, I had to assess men with my head. I could not afford to be swept away on a tide of passion . . . and my instincts told me . . . that I had to be a winner.

Lehar's reputation was that of his famous song . . . 'Girls were made to love and kiss . . ' with the final line of his song saying 'And I'll kiss them wherever I can . . '.

This enigmatic old man was now mine to explore, how incredible? So much had already been written about him all over the world, that I felt sure that he would make the same mark in history as had Johann Strauss, Schubert and Mozart. But what about me? I thought. Was this to be my cresendo to fame? Why should I be discreet or diplomatic? Why not let all Vienna know about his roving eyes? Why not shout it from the roof-tops . . . . what womanly weapons should I use to bedazzle him, to play just one song with his own hands? I know we all have five senses but my sensuality added another, as Professor Fischer declared, that any man who remained unaware of it, would have to be dumb and blind.

Lehar conjured up a new world for me . . . . a challenge, and I prepared myself to rise to the occasion, as a flower rises to the sun. Suddenly, I wanted to know everything about this great man, his possible behaviour, the truth about the crazy rumours that surrounded him, his supposed womanising, and dismissals when spurned. At least where I was concerned, he was not dealing with a girl from the gutter, but the young Baroness Haan, whose family upheld a tradition, befitting the Royal House of Habsburg.

My unassailable logic, sometimes confused me; for men would be men, and I should have known better having tasted and discarded them. My aim was to be the top star in Vienna and transcend all obstacles with confidence and to hear the immortal words of Franz Lehar saying to me: "You will stay in my memory and linger on."

Indeed Lehar had risen to my temptation and told me: "You radiate passion and excitement my girl, you have the right kind of armoury, a benevolent sexual tension, to get what you want."

It appeared that I was all women to all men. But, who would not have been impressed to be courted by a world-famous man, like Franz Lehar? All I could think about, was our meeting. Bubbling over with success and happiness, I got to bed; but sleep would not come easily, as I wondered how much of this evening had been real and how much had been superficial. This night, however, will stay in my mind through my entire life.

After a long lie-in, I bathed, dressed and began to examine my floral tributes, which had all been delivered to the house. There were all kinds of intriguing messages enclosed, ranging from offers for a one-night stand, to invitations for charity events, through to dinner dates.

However, the long-stemmed dark red roses were from Lehar, and the card read: "*Schatz, ich bitt Dich, komm heut Nacht*", with a request to phone him, also giving his ex-directory number. "Dearest I beg you come tonight", it read and I recalled his daring look as he kissed my hand and wondered if he had ever been rejected by a woman.

Yet, curiosity got the better of me and I telephoned him. His housekeeper answered and called him to the phone. For seconds, neither of us talked, until Lehar finally broke the silence and said: "I sensed it was you, but we will have to be discreet. You know that I have a wife, although we lead our separate lives in our castle, the walls have ears, and maybe waiting for just such an opportunity as this, to create a scandal."

I paused at this revelation, and became unsure about what I should reply, but need not have worried as Lehar did not even give me the opportunity, insisting that his driver would collect me the following evening at 8 p.m. and then he hung the phone up.

What a strange man, and how mysterious! Here was new adventure beckoning, putting me in a right old tizzy!

When I told my aunt about my telephone conversation, or rather lack of it, with the great man, she had a good laugh and exclaimed: "Lehar is old enough to be your grandfather and even though known as a Romeo, *par exellence*, is really no threat to you. At least you will have the satisfaction, to one day tell your children, that the maestro desired you."

Was this really what I wanted? To pretend to this old, but great man that I was his for the asking just so that my ambitions and vanity would be fed? Upon examining my reasons, I found, that if I were honest with myself, a small part of me could not resist such an ego boost, but the larger part of my personality was merely curious and eager to learn a little more about the man who had given me already so much pleasure with his songs, many of which were my favourites. So I determined to defend myself, should the old fox, try anything funny with me, mainly because I wanted to keep the great respect I had for him, as a composer. And I truly believed, that it would have saddened me to find that the man fell short of the heights that the composer had achieved.

Flowers kept arriving all day long, until the scent of the lovely blooms permiated every corner of the house. Captain Bass also called, bringing us some more goodies, and offered to drive me to the Vienna Woods, to get some fresh air as the house smelled like a perfume factory.

This was the best suggestion that I had been offered in a long time. It was so peaceful and serene there, that all the worries and complications of life disappeared. With Captain Bass next to me, assuring me of his personal attention, who could have asked for more? I was surrounded with men and success, and should really not have had a care in the world, yet it was the shrewd face of Lehar's that would not leave my mind. As the excitement of the last twenty-four hours began to well up inside me, I began to look forward to eight o'clock and my clandestine rendezvous with the man, whose music was famous the world over.

Charged with anticipation of the unknown, I entered his 'Rosenschlossel', and indeed, Lehar did not disappoint me, and never crushed my belief in him as he proved to me that the man, was as great as the composer.

"His 'Castle of Roses', as it was named, was outside the city of Vienna and well hidden from the probing eye of the public. I had no doubt that the rumours about his various affairs were quite true, as the setting of his home lent itself perfectly to such a life. No doubt, many a young lady had left via the back door unnoticed, happy in the knowledge, that his word would ensure her a contract or even a role, that she desired.

I, however, fancied that I was rather different to them, as Lehar had known the Baron Haans very well, and thus would most certainly have to treat me with good manners and etiquette. As I was standing there in the hall, I also began to remind myself that there was no need for panic, as surely at the ripe-old age of seventy-two, Lehar's earthly repertoire of love-making had come to an end in a physical sense. I calmed myself with the thought that it was only natural that his manly vanity still wanted to be surrounded by beautiful women.

As he came towards me, to greet me, he studied me from head to toe and said: "You look so ridiculously young Burgi, that I am glad, that the light is low; at least you will not be able to see all the lines on my face."

At that moment, I must admit that I felt rather sad for him . . . . the great man realistic of his age . . . so, to lift his morale, I told him that the lines on his face made him distinguished looking, and that I would hear no more talk of age, as I had come to cheer him up and to sing for him.

"Good, then let's get on with it," was his smiling reply, as he led me into a beautiful room with a grand piano. He seated himself on the piano stool, and began playing the introduction to the 'Czarewitsch'. "*Warum hat jeder Frühling auch nur einen Mai . . . warum bleibt dir das dumme Herz nicht ewig treu?*" "Why has every springtime only ever one May . . . . why can this silly heart not remain faithful forever?"

Indeed very apt for Lehar, as many Mays had passed him by, but at least, he had the harvest of his enchanting music, safely tucked away in his bank account. Yet, his private life was far from happy, according to my aunt, consequently the many discreet, only whispered about his diversions.

Additionally, a man like him, was of course always fair game for the scandal merchants, and of course also ran the risk of blackmail.

Whilst these and other thoughts were rushing through my mind, trying to get an impression of the man behind the talent, Lehar, probably realising that my mind was not in the song that I was singing, suggested a break and said: "Let's have something to eat."

We went into the next room, and sat down at a nicely arranged supper-table, which was bedecked with cold meats and salads and had also two bottles of champagne in an ice cooler, standing on it. I was in my element, with all that lovely food. Franz, lit two candles and looked at me. I could not help but return his gaze and noted that his eyes had definitely something crafty about them. They were a grey-blue, set in a broad face with a strong chin. It struck me as odd that I so admired the composer, yet could find nothing in the face of the man that I could warm to. He was simply Franz Lehar, a brilliant man, but there could never be any more. I wondered then whether I should tell him, what went through my mind, but decided that discretion would be the better part of valour. After all, who could tell what the future held. Maybe he would want to help me to reach the top of my profession. If he really considered me a good singer, perhaps he would even promote me? . . . There was no point in making an enemy of such a powerful man, just for the sake of being able to say . . . . that I was the one, who really told him what I thought of him.

We talked mainly about the theatre and the opera house in Vienna, which had nearly been destroyed completely by fire, and how sad the loss of the costumes were, as the Volkstheatre now had to cope with makeshift scenery and costumes, and third-rate actors.

During our conversation Lehar also explained, what he considered important and his words were immediately committed to memory for ever as he said: "Always sing your main songs centre stage, and upright, I cannot bear a singer to sit and sing. And when you kiss on stage . . . . always remember to make it real . . . . never mind the damn make-up."

I had to laugh, but soon had that smile wiped off my face, when he got hold of me and gave me a demonstration of how a kiss should be. This was not meant to be a rehearsal, but appeared to me more like a man losing control of himself.

Although I had no wish to upset the man, I decided that diplomatic relations had run their course and that the time for truth had come. I put him straight in a polite but firm manner, thanking him for the compliment he had paid my feminine ego, but reminding him that this was entirely out of place between friends, explaining that I had truly come to cheer him up, because I admired his works enormously, but that personal feelings really did not enter into it.

He then smilingly replied: "You are teasing me with sex in your head, versus sex in my body, and I must admit that the latter is on its last leg."

My rendezvous with Lehar was over, and he escorted me to the car and handed me an orchid in a box, on which he had written: "Thank you, for being you".

I lived in an aura of austerity, and had been able to sample the best life had to offer. My route had taken me through the hearts of many men, but when I left Lehar, I was more convinced then ever that love dominated all, no matter how hard and tough men pretended to be, their lives could be made or broken by it.

As the driver took me home through the streets of the city, I saw

Vienna for the first time as it really was. Corrupt, with girls walking the streets, hunting every type of uniform. It was the uniformed men, who had, what these girls wanted, more than anything else in the world . . . . FOOD! The Yanks, in particular were in high fashion, as they had the most to give. And the British slogan for them, which was . . . . OVERPAID AND OVERSEXED, applied quite well.

Raw sex to me was awful as I needed to be in love first and foremost. So the only thing that differentiated me from those poor girls, was that I had adopted a wait and see policy, as the wisdom of Lehar's song replayed in my ear: "*Einer wird kommen, dem werd ich gehören* . . . . " "One day, a man will come . . . to whom I'll belong . . . forever."

Even though this may have been naive, I knew that when the right man came along, I would recognise him when he kissed me.

As the city lights were flickering past, I began in my mind to examine the people around me. The two main characters were really Ell and Captain Bass, on whose friendship, not only I, but also my relatives depended, for the food on our table. I concluded that without a firm offer, my ideals and stage ambitions would have to be shelved temporarily, until I could secure a contract that would enable me to live on my own and make me independent of the hand-outs from Captain Bass and Corporal Ell.

The situation, as it was, demanded that three ration books supplied enough food for four people. As the rations were barely enough to keep just those three, it was definitely impossible to feed four. So I had no alternative but to keep Corporal Ell and Captain Bass sweet, in order to merely survive.

I arrived home exhausted and thought that I would sleep forever; but when my head hit the pillow, my mind would not give in, as the present irony of the situation I found myself in, replayed itself over and over again. The biggest annoyance was that even if I could earn money on a regular basis with my singing and acting, it still would not get me very far, as most shops had next to nothing to sell anyway.

An example of this had been last week's supply of food, which we had obtained by conventional means, i.e. over the shop counter. For the four of us, it had amounted to a quarter of kg of bread, four eggs, a quarter of a pound of butter and a little meat, which had been obtained from the black market, at a price. The latter was big business and really the only way to survive.

The more I thought about it, the more awake I became, as anger welled up inside of me. The old and poor perished . . . and no-one cared. All around me there were people starving, and I saw my best friends giving away the most fabulous jewellery, that they had managed to hide from the Nazis, in exchange for a few pounds of flour, some sugar and one kg of goulash — meat.

Counting all the injustices in the world, I finally fell into a deep sleep, lifting the burden, from my young shoulders.

Some days later, there developed an almighty row in the house over just such an incident. My cousin Nelly, had handed over a diamond-studded watch, given to her by her late grandmother, for a few items of food and some cigarettes. My aunt was horrified by what she had done, telling her in the strongest terms that she must never do anything like it again.

Adding to this upset, was the fact that Corporal Ell, left a note saying that he would not be able to come and see us as frequently as he had done, as all his time was once again taken up driving the brigadier, here, there and everywhere, adding that if I wanted food, he would collect me after he had taken the brigadier and let me share his own food ration at the barracks.

As he was unable to bring us any more food, this then seemed to be the next best solution. So after he had delivered the brigadier to his home or to a party, he would take me to Kitchener Barracks, where he would collect his food and give it to me to eat in the back of the car.

I had certainly come a long way. Here I was, eighteen months after Austria had been liberated, hiding in a British car, in a barrack yard, eating fish and chips out of an army metal container. 'God have mercy on us Austrians,' I thought 'and send us something to eat soon, before we lose our dignity as a nation altogether and start camping outside the various military establishments like beggars, or worse, before we become a nation of prostitutes, soliciting men for food.'

I vowed to myself, that I would never go as far as the latter, as my body was the only thing that still belonged to me. And I swore, then and there, to myself that no-one would be allowed to have fun with it, just for the sake of some food; I would starve first.

As the days passed by, Corporal Ell became very concerned about my welfare and suggested that we should get engaged, which would enable him to get a flat for me and care for me. He assured me that until we were married, he would sleep at his army quarters and visit me a weekends. Even though this was not what I had imagined for myself, it was the only solution for me at the time. So I agreed and started looking for somewhere to rent, when 'Lady Luck' threw the answer into my lap almost by accident.

Professor Fischer had heard that his next-door neighbour was eager to let a flat, and so I telephoned him the next day, thus killing two birds with one stone, as I could go just across the corridor for my singing lessons, thus saving me the long journey from the 18th district, where I had been living with my aunt.

Although my aunt was not overjoyed at this news, she had to agree, that it was best for all, certainly as far as my career was concerned. Professor Fischer had valuable contacts . . . . , which eventually would enable me to earn my own living.

Suddenly my life began to have meaning once more. Professor Fischer, introduced me to some very influential agents and artists, one of whom was the great Herbert Thöny. He became the catalyst, creating exciting opportunities for me, alas not selflessly, I had to admit. So I began 'stringing' him along, as he promised that the world would be my oyster, if I played my cards right. Little did he know that I was a past master at this game. Thus, Thöny, took me to all the important parties, blazing the trail for my success. Indeed, the VIPs did take notice and I was asked to play the lead in Lehar's 'Merry Widow'.

Rehearsals began at once and poor Corporal Ell, had to play second fiddle, to all the comings and goings in the flat, that he paid for. However, he was so generous, and with his endless patience, I began to think of him as a martyr to my cause. He would just casually drop in and leave without fuss, if he saw that I was busy with my rehearsals.

The weeks just flew by and it finally appeared that by December 1946, I had my own life in a strict embrace, and my survival instincts on the essential tasks in hand. I was quite happy with my new disciplined life and the fact that I had managed to conquer my restless and disorganised spirit.

However this atmosphere was not to prevail for long, as fate, in which I now believed wholeheartedly decided to pull the carpet from under my feet.

News reached me, that my mother was dangerously ill, and that I would have to go to St. Michael at once if I wanted to see her alive. The shock of these unexpected turn of events was sufficient to rock the very foundations of the finely balanced scales, that I had started to build my new life on. On top of the upset I felt, was the added difficulty of getting back home fast. St. Michael was some 200 km away, which meant crossing the awkward Semering border again, although this time I did have a pass; but now no transport. Corporal Ell was unable to assist, as his duties lay in Vienna with

Brigadier Templer, thus I was on my own in finding some other means.

The answer to my problems, however, was not as difficult as I had anticipated. Captain Elliott, the manager of the theatre, suggested a lift with a Major Chappelle. When I asked if he was French, I was told "No, he is British." This rather disappointed me as I had momentarily been curious to find out how the fourth occupation power behaved, especially, as I had already experienced the other three.

However, there was no time to lose, so I packed only the essentials in clothing, plus food and fruit, in the hope that these would aid in my mother's recovery, and waited for the arrival of Chappelle's car.

Punctually, he came and very formally introduced himself as he helped me into his chauffeur-driven car.

The journey went quite well with light conversation flowing easily, when Major Chappelle suddenly, during a moment when I was looking out of the window, began exploring my figure with his hands. I had to remind him that I had not come with him on a joy-ride, but that I was visiting my seriously ill mother.

He simply replied: "Well more the fool me then, I believed dear Elliott, when he told me that you were a real sexy lady, and not some frosty Fräulein."

I could have hit him, but as I did not want to walk the next 150 km, I decided to grit my teeth and almost smilingly replied, "I am afraid that you are a little too fast for my tastes. After all I only met you an hour ago; I prefer my men to woe me a little longer than that, as this raw and primitive approach does nothing for me."

Chappelle's steel-blue eyes obviously expected a different reply, and for a couple of moments it looked as if I would end up walking after all. But he must have decided to try his luck on the way back and returned to the easy banter of conversation we had shared before this unfortunate incident. The rest of the journey went all right if travelling with a pipe-smoking octopus can be considered 'alright'. The fumes in the car were awful, and I was glad for the fresh air when we arrived.

During the journey, I had sized him up and had found that he stood for everything I disliked in a man, but I had no option; I dared not offend him outright, as he was also my ticket back to Vienna. Thus, I hinted at a possible romance, on our return to Vienna and even quoted to him "That all was fair in love and war".

He replied: "You are too clever by half, but I am intrigued and accept your proposal."

Indeed he then insisted on coming along to see my mother. I wondered what went on under the exterior of such a man, but was soon returned to the present, when I saw how desperately ill my mother really was. She could hardly speak and really did look, as if she was on her deathbed.

I was desperately worried and began shouting at the neighbour who was looking after her: "We must get proper help, or she will die before our eyes."

Chappelle was openly moved by my plight, and immediately offered to drive me to Leoben, where the nearest hospital was, to see if they would take care of her. Just as we got up to do that, the local doctor arrived, whom the neighbour had already called. Had I given her a chance to explain, she would no doubt have told me, but as usual, I had gone overboard. I apologised to the neighbour, who kindly offered to make us some tea, while the doctor went to examine my mother. When he came out of her room I asked him still hopeful, what her chances of recovery were?

He sadly replied: "I am sorry, they are nil, it's now only a matter of time, at most a matter of a few weeks. I am truly sorry, there is nothing that I, or anyone can do for her now."

As the gravity of his words sank into my brain, tears just streamed down my face.

My mother's neighbour put her arms around me saying: "You have got to be strong now, your mum knows, and she is taking it better than you are. Don't fret yourself, she is in good hands, I am a retired nurse, and I spend every day with her until your stepfather comes home and then he looks after her. Which reminds me, he will be home any time now."

This was enough to bring me back out of my stupor, and I thanked her kindly saying that I wished to talk with my mother alone now. I went into her room and kneeled down by her bed. I took her frail hands and kissed them asking: "Oh Mother, what shall I do now?"

She replied: "Go back to Vienna, study hard, and make me proud of you. There is nothing that you or anyone can do for me, and don't worry yourself, I am in good hands, and when I leave this earth I will be in even better hands. And remember wherever you are singing, one day, I am sure God will let me watch. So go, do your best and make me proud of you."

I kissed her hands, for the last time and left the room just as my stepfather arrived home. He greeted me warmly and assured me that he would look after my mother, and with that I asked Major Chappelle to drive me back.

A rather subdued major, sat with me in the back of the car, now keeping his hands well to himself, as we headed back to Vienna with me in floods of tears.

Shaking with grief, Professor Fischer embraced me, when I got back and told me, that it was vital now to bring some purpose into my life. It's always hard on those that are left behind, but discipline, is the first step towards leading a normal life again, and that in my case discipline would be the first step towards success, which was after all what my mother had wanted for me.

So after a few days, I pulled myself together and started to follow Professor Fischer's orders to the letter. Discipline was now my daily diet. Soon I became an image of a perfectly groomed actress and singer, with people watching me when I left the house — just to see what I was wearing that day. I became a little like an automatic machine. Men friends came and went, but none were ever allowed to stay the night. I had begun to live in a superficial bubble, no-one really mattered, the only thing that remained to form a link between me and the real world, was my singing and acting career. Subconsciously, I had cut myself off from everyone. Grief can take many forms, in my case it shaped me into trying to be the daughter that I suspected my mother had always longed for, instead of the selfish, sometimes thoughtless, and even reckless girl I had actually been. Ironically, discipline had been the keyword to it all. I would not even allow poor Ell into my world any more. He was in love with me alright, above and beyond the call of duty, yet all I wanted, was companionship, whilst all he wanted, was to marry me.

As time went by, I eventually extricated myself out of my superficial bubble and joined the land of the living again. Even though I had always put off the inevitable, the time had come to give some serious consideration to Ell's proposal. So I began weighing up the odds. I desperately needed financial security. If I married Ell, I would then become a British subject, this would entitle me to many privileges, free lodgings and of course regular food rations. However, the more I thought about it, the more indecisive I became. As there was no desperate hurry for an immediate decision, I simply decided to leave the matter hanging in the air, for a while longer.

The following weeks passed fairly uneventfully, until the middle of June 1946, when I finally got a singing engagement with the British Forces Network, through Captain Elliott, who was now with ENSA, and arranged and organised all the entertainment for the troops in Austria. The most memorable moment of that time was my audition. I applied at the same time, as a girl called Mitzi Gerbler. I can still hear his supercilious remarks about her, as he said to his colleague: "That girl has got the perfect legs for a dancer, ... but as for anything else . . . . . far too little on top."

At the time I wondered whether he was referring to her bust or brain, either of which would have been an insult. Little did he know then, that she would go on and become famous as the replacement for Betty Grable, when 20th Century Fox snapped her up, and renamed her Mitzi Gaynor. I would have given anything, to see him eat his words then.

From the moment I was engaged by him for the network, Captain Elliott began following me around with all sorts of offers. Although, I found him interesting and pleasant, he was not my cup of tea, rather shark-like, and completely oblivious, that he was making a nuisance of himself.

Yet I had no means of shaking him off as my working for him meant our travelling together to Klagenfurt, near the Italian border, where I was to commence on a singing tour. Even though on that occasion Corporal Ell was also travelling with me, his first duty lay with the brigadier, whom he had to tend to first, thus still leaving me for several hours alone in the company of Captain Elliott. It would have been fair to assume, that as I was travelling with my fiance, this would put an end to the amorous advances of the captain. But not so, I had to remind him several times, that I was now engaged to Corporal Ell.

This however, did little to deter him as he finally in blatant frustration said to me: "You can say what you like, you can even marry your Corporal Ell, but it is *I* who will be making love to you . . . ".

Whatever next I thought, the Liberators certainly lived by a strange code of behaviour. As he was my employer however, I decided to play him along at his own little game. Our stay at the beautiful Wörthersee had its moments. I spent the better part of my free time, keeping Captain Elliott at elbows' length and out of Corporal Ell's sight, as he was of the opinion, that I already saw far too much of him at work. This was all very well, but I could hardly stop him turning up at the villa, where he invariably managed to manoeuvre me out of Corporal Ell's way under some pretext, or other.

The funniest occasion, was when he insisted on taking me on a moonlight excursion on the lake which had a little island in the centre of it. The villa where we stayed, had its own boat-house, as the lake flowed right past the perimeter of the property.

Although, my heart was really not in this, I agreed to keep the peace. Luckily, the boat sprang a leak as we were nearly half-way to the island. As the boat, just filled up with water, with either of us being unable to do anything about it, it finally sank, so we swam for the shore. His ardour considerably dampened, the captain emerged soaked through to the skin, much to my suppressed amusement. I fetched him a cloth, to at least dry his head off, yet he had no choice, but to walk back to his lodgings, dripping wet. No doubt, he would tell his fellow officers some tall story, but why should I care?

Those were the days . . . . . and upon my return to Vienna, this whole episode soon came to an end, with me much wiser now . . . in dealing with men on my terms only.

March 1947.

My mother had died. We buried her in St. Michael, under a blanket of deep snow. Although I was wearing a warm coat, I was shivering on the arms of an old friend, a Dr Heinz Moser. He was the only son of a most distinguished medical family from Leoben. It was he, who held me upright, as the coffin with my alpine flower wreath was lowered into the grave.

While the priest gave his closing comments, I wondered if I could not have made her life a little easier, if I had been less of a rebel and more of a devoted daughter. Unfortunately, it was too late now.

I glanced over at my stepfather, but he just looked on motionless. When the ceremony was over, however, he came over, embraced me and said how sorry he was, for all that had happened. I was drained of tears and emotions, and merely said that it was too late for regrets now anyway. He said goodbye and left.

As I looked around me and saw the handful of mourners departing from the cemetery, it struck me as very sad, that so few had turned up to pay their last respects, even though, she had been such a kind and generous woman, who had aided so many. It was only the opulent amount of flowers, that somehow paid tribute to the kind of person she had been, in their way compensating for the poor attendance.

Heinz and I were the last to leave the graveside. As we were walking through the cemetery gates, he invited me to have lunch with him at a nearby hotel. On our way there we talked about my mother, whom he liked very much and had often visited during my absence, when he was on leave from his army duties, as a doctor.

Over lunch, he enquired what my plans for the future were, and if I intended to go to England? He added emotionally, that I would always have a home in the beautiful house of his parents, who had also known my mother very well. Then to my utter amazement, he said: "I am afraid, I cannot offer you anything the British can give you, only the love of a poor Austrian doctor."

I interpreted this as his way of comforting me. I then explained, that I would be returning to Vienna, but thanking him for his kind offer. I added that I had received the star role in the most lavish revue staged since the war, called the 'Maske in Blau, and that I would do my best to fulfil my mother's wish in making her proud of me.

He wished me the best of luck, kissed my hand and we parted.

Upon my return to Vienna, I had a pistol to my head, in the form of bills, including the bill for my mother's funeral, which my stepfather had not even the decency to pay. So when Corporal Ell asked me for the second time to marry him, I said yes, as there was no other option open to me. We fixed the date for the 8th May, as Corporal Ell knew that his posting back to the UK, was imminent.

The wedding, turned into a social event, with the grandson of the Princess of Liechtenstein, offering to be Corporal Ell's best man. He was of course a relative of mine, by the name of Dr Zdenko Peithner. He was actually Czech, like my mother, and wore the decorations befitting a nobleman. Other guests included barons, the von Schrack family, a leading barrister, Dr Walter Schuppich, my aunt Jenny, the Baroness von Haan and Uncle Otto von Haan, my cousins Mitzi & Nelly, and the Countess Navratil, who owned the Villa of Count Turn and Taxis, where the reception was being held.

A small band played and gold braided waiters stood at the ready to look after our guests which amounted to approximately twenty-five.

The excellent food was supplied by the staff of Kitchener Barracks, including the beautiful wedding-cake, which was a work of art.

I felt like a vandal when I cut the cake, but my hungry guests could hardly wait to get their teeth into it, with my new husband remarking: "That food obviously made them forget their aristocratic upbringing."

This rather hasty remark was, merely a prelude of what was to come. I however, gritted my teeth and remained charming. Corporal Ell and the NCOs began drinking heavily, and inevitably with intoxication, they began to show off, and one had the audacity to shout: "When the vultures have finished eating, they can clear off . . . . . perhaps we can get on with our party then?"

I was dumbfounded, as a stony silence fell over the room. The hallowed dignity of my marriage was over.

I left, without my husband, by the back door and returned to our flat in the 3rd district.

Still furious, I undressed, locked the door and went to bed.

My new husband, however, did not come home until the following morning. Realising that he had been in the wrong, he apologised over and over again. I accepted his apology, but our marriage now resembled a broken mirror. Despite this fact, we went on a short honeymoon in the brigadier's car, which had been his contribution. The use of the car was greatly appreciated, as it gave us the opportunity to visit my grandmother in Graz, some old friends in the country, and my mother's grave in St. Michael.

My grandmother, however, was very angry, over my decision of marriage to Corporal Ell, and she forecast that this arrangement would never stand the test of time, in fact, she said that it would be over, by the end of the year.

She was right! When we returned from our honeymoon, my husband left almost immediately with the brigadier for Prague; which left me happily to my own devices for a few weeks. I continued my singing lessons and met with my friends, of whom my husband, now so disapproved, happy in the knowledge that he was far away, unable to embarrass me.

When he returned, however, he began to indulge in heavy drinking sessions with his pals, and openly abused anyone who came to our flat. It got to the point, where people dreaded coming around, until eventually we became almost social outcasts, because of his unreasonable behaviour.

When my husband finally left for England, it was a great relief, not only for me but also for my family. As I kissed him goodbye, I knew that our marriage was over.

I moved to a bigger flat in strange surroundings to make a fresh start. All my concentration went into my singing and acting career, and any spare time was spent in making the flat, as cosy as possible. After my husband had gone to England, my cousins Mitzi and Nelly begged me to move back into their house, but with my newly-found freedom, I had no intention to subject myself to the watchful eyes of my relatives again, so I declined their well meant offer.

But, alas, my new landlady died quite unexpectedly, which gave me all of one month to find a new place of residence.

As I was determined to keep my independence, I went to see my husband's welfare officer, a Captain Hunter, who advised me to make an appointment with a Major Protheroe. This I immediately did.

It was now the 1st of September 1947.

It was a beautiful autumn morning as I began to dress for my forthcoming meeting with Major Protheroe. After a fair amount of indecision I finally decided to wear a light grey, fitted two piece with navy accessories, topped with a hat, that was very chic. It was the height in fashion, and the last word in 'haute couture', decorated with a large satin bow on the back of the brim. Casually, I flung my red fox furs over my shoulders and left the flat.

In the street I hailed a taxi to take me to the Reissnerstrasse. As I got out of the taxi, a friend of mine, a lady called Maria, stopped me to ask whom I was going to meet dressed like, I was. I explained to her that I was going to see a Major Protheroe, as I would soon be without a roof over my head, in the hope that he would help me find some living accommodation.

She laughed as she replied: "You will get somewhere to live alright, but if you're not careful you'll end up with the major as your lodger."

Ignoring her teasing I bade her farewell, as I would be late for my appointment if I did not hurry and made my way up the steps of the British Consulate.

I stated my name and reason for being there to the clerk, who took me straight into the major's office. The man behind the desk, looked up, and rather startled by my elegant appearance, jumped to his feet, and introduced himself as Major E. Protheroe.

As the clerk left the room, he asked me to take a seat and enquired smilingly what he could do for me? His smile exuded such a warmth and his eyes had such a hypnotic quality about them, that I was temporarily lost for words.

Transfixed, by this unexpected vision before me, I just gazed at him unable to think. In fact, we just gazed at each other until finally his rich deep voice filtered through to my brain where I could hear him say: "Please excuse me for staring, but that ridiculous hat, suits you so well, that I just can't seem to take my eyes of it."

Still spellbound I replied: "I am not surprised, it's supposed to have that effect; it's the new Marlene Dietrich fashion!" With that remark I turned my head to give him a full view of this quite exquisite creation.

His presence somehow, totally captivated me, and before I knew what was happening, I had completely fallen under his spell. The major's now, blatantly flirtatious manner increased, as he complimented me on my outfit. I told him that I was a singer, and that I hoped to make it my career.

"In London?" he asked.

So we began a conversation, which had absolutely nothing to do with my reasons for seeing him.

After a while, he ordered his clerk to bring us a pot of tea. When the clerk brought the tea, Protheroe, pretended to be sifting through some papers, but I knew where his thoughts really were with me. The clerk left, giving me the oddest look! After all, a whole hour had passed and I was still sitting there.

How could one possibly drift into this kind of situation? Obviously selfish instincts, to the exclusion of all other prevailed, as we became two lost souls, hungry for adventure.

I was simply too much of a temptation for this man, and with my perfume in the air, a cloud lifted us into oblivion.

"By the way, my name is Eric," said he, as he removed my fox furs from my shoulders. He stood so close that I could feel his breath on my face as he added: "From the moment, you walked into my office . . . . I wanted to kiss you. Does that shock you Mrs Ell?"

Of course it did, but the man had such an hypnotic affect on me that I was unable to utter a single word. I stood there dumbfounded, almost paralysed whilst Major Protheroe caressed my neck. We both trembled with abandonment of all senses, powered by a passion, beyond our human control.

Was it really possible, that the legal administrator would risk all for a few hours of passion? And more to the point, could such a thing really happen in Her Majesty's Consulate?

Similar thoughts must have gone through Protheroe's mind, for he finally sat down behind his desk and began reading my husband's letter, who was now living in Newmarket with his father, a former jockey, training racehorses. Although the letter said little, it contained the vital line which stated that my husband was unable to find us a flat, and that it might be better for me to wait a little longer before I joined him. This last sentence was vital to my gaining an extension of stay in Vienna. After reading the letter completely, Protheroe made a few telephone calls and eventually turned to me and said "I managed to get you a room in the British Transit Hotel, Astoria. Will that do?"

My joy was twofold but I was afraid to express it, as with every gesture and word, we came closer. As all formalities had ceased to exist we were only waiting for 5 p.m. to come, when he would be released from his duty at the Consulate. It seemed as if his secretary was the only sane person around now, when she interrupted our anxious wait, by bringing in a mountain of paperwork, which he attended in a nervous manner. She looked at me suspiciously, as he was signing the documents, probably because of the length of time that I had been there. The major however, noticed nothing!

When she had left the room, he arranged to take me to my hotel, pre-empting this with a visit to my flat, enabling me to collect some of my things. All of this was directed towards us spending some time on our own together. The clock chimed five, and we left blatantly arm in arm. We flew down the official staircase, and into his car. He drove himself, making the tension between us unbearable. When we arrived at my flat, Frau Hiller, the servant greeted us and offered to bring part of my luggage downstairs. I looked at him and had to smile, when I saw Protheroe's face. The obvious look of disappointment at the thwarting of his plan by a kind servant was enough to try his patience.

Yet, when the woman shouted *"küss die hand"*; we both laughed, and he insisted that I explained its meaning. It was an Austrian custom of reverence, a hint to give a tip.

He immediately replied "Oh I understand, but if you give me your hands, I will kiss them for the pleasure of it." Subsequently, we drove off en route to the Hotel Astoria, which was to become my home for the next six months. The major again reminded me to call him Eric, saying that it was long overdue. However, when I tried to copy him, it sounded like Erich. This made him laugh and the game of teasing and love had begun. Was it an adventure leading to ecstasy, or despair?

This is madness Erich," I said.

But he merely replied "No, it's quite simple. A stranger entered my office and two lovers left it."

How could I possibly reason with a man like him, who was prepared to risk his position. I hated myself for being so weak and vulnerable, allowing yet another stranger to dominate my life.

The Hotel Astoria was situated in the best part of Vienna, and was bettered only by the Hotel Sacher, which with its delicious 'Sachertorte', had a reputation, that was unrivalled anywhere. It was a sheer luxury few could afford. Yet, Major Protheroe invited me to dine there, after he had registered me at the Astoria. I happily agreed.

In the sequence of events that was to follow, it was a foregone conclusion, that we would end up in each other's arms. Consequently — when we returned from our meal, we entered the foyer of the Astoria, as if we were married. The receptionist was very polite, whilst Major Protheroe did all the talking and signing of the register. We were given the key to number 21, and the porter was ordered to take up my cases. The major hesitated momentarily, over whether we should take the lift or walk. Furthermore it was written all over his face, whether he should say goodbye now and leave, or whether he should take the next step towards an affair. He obviously decided for the latter, and we walked upstairs past the many mirrors, which now reflected in me a guilty feeling.

When we reached my room, Eric picked me up and carried me over the doorstep, putting me down slowly, but not letting go of me, as he said "You have taken away my senses dear Burgi, and if being so happy is a sin, then let us be sinners." In between kisses he uttered "What more can I say to you my darling?"

He took off my ridiculous hat, and kissed me without self-control, until I wrenched myself free. I simply had to stop him, as this all or nothing business was too much for me, and I told him so. Eric apologised and promised to be more patient.

We changed the conversation as to what I should wear for dinner, and I held up a midnight-blue silk dress, asking for his opinion?

He nodded an affirmative, as the telephone rang. It was the receptionist, wishing to know if we were dining at the hotel, in order that she might reserve a table for us. I declined, thanking her for her concern, wondering if she had guessed what was going on?

Protheroe decided to leave, so that he could get changed for the evening, and I was glad to be alone to sort out my wardrobe, but most of all to have some time to think. My idealism did not mix with the special treatment now offered to me, and I felt that it was wrong to accept that kind of love, which had strings attached to it. However, the night was young, and I dressed, choosing a different gown to the one I had held up in front of Major Protheroe. I decided on an off-the-shoulder dress, which had a two-tier skirt, drawing attention to my slim legs and small feet.

It was now 6.30 p.m., and a knock at my door made me jump. However, it was only the receptionist going off duty, who introduced herself as Kamilla, who wished me an enjoyable stay.

"How nice of you," I remarked, whilst examining myself in the full-length mirror.

Her dark eyes surveyed me cheekily, as she said "Well looking like you do, it's no wonder that the major looks bewitched and bewildered my dear."

I did not quite know how to take that, but assured her that we were only good friends!

As she was shutting the door, I heard her reply "Now where did I hear that excuse before?" It was obvious that nothing escaped Kamilla, so why worry myself?

The man under whose spell I had fallen was to collect me in an hour, and every minute from now on, felt like an eternity. Every time I heard a footstep in the corridor my heart began to race. At last they were his. He arrived with a bunch of carnations, attired in his best uniform, which enhanced his perfect figure, and broad shoulders. As I was now wearing a different dress, he enquired how I had managed to get such lovely clothes in post-war Vienna.

I told him "Of course via the black market, selling my food and mainly cigarettes to the highest bidder."

Eric laughed exclaiming "It's incredible what lengths women will go to, in order to feed their vanity, but why not? You look lovely." He took me into his arms, crushing my skirt and kissed me until I was breathless.

How outrageously daring I thought, there was nothing cool about this Englishman, and it appeared that he had abandoned all codes of etiquette.

I also found out that he was quite a romantic, when he told me in words that any girl would like to hear "Darling, it is written in your eyes, what your lips cannot tell me, but I understand."

We walked daringly downstairs, passed another receptionist and the manager, who wished us a pleasant evening with a twinkle in his eye. It was then that I realised, that what we were doing was just taken for granted under the circumstances. We once again opted for the Hotel Sacher, which was practically next door, all lit up and extremely elegant. The manager a colonel, came to greet us. I was rather nervous, fiddling with my glittering evening bag, as some ladies were staring at me. However, we were soon ushered out of their sight, and shown to a special table reserved for VIPs. I was immediately faced with the scrutiny of Protheroe's fellow officers, but the former remarked "Darling, they would give their right arm, to be in my place, eat, drink and be merry, for tomorrow we may be dead."

"What a thing to say" I answered, but he explained about his war years, and how close he had been to being killed, which suddenly made me realise that we had something in common. The ex-combat major had come alive, with tales of his war experiences, yet he prevented me from talking about my resistance days. We ordered trout and vegetables, plus a bottle of claret from the à la carte menu, and toasted each other, with Eric suggesting that after the meal, we should get a taxi and go to the Officers' Club "Am Graben", in the centre of Vienna.

When we arrived there, the dancing was in full swing and the place was crowded, but nothing mattered to us, as we could be together and enjoy the evening. The band was playing softly 'You do something to me . . . something to hypnotise me . . . ', and Protheroe took me into his arms and we danced and sang together

'You do something to me, nobody else can do'.

We knew we were lost, enslaved in a liaison, which was forbidden and wrong, but who could stop this burning desire in our hearts and bodies? It's so easy for outsiders not involved, to criticise and condemn, but in this room full of hundreds of people, mostly officers, there were only two people who mattered . . . us. I realised that several officers acknowledged Eric, but he seemed oblivious.

We decided to walk back to our hotel, a little bit tipsy and laughing. My high heels got caught between the cobbled stones, which made my major insist on carrying me, stumbling most of the way, to the amusement of passers-by. I was around eight stone in weight, but "featherlite" as Eric insisted, yet he stumbled even more, at which we collapsed with laughter, at our antics. The closer we came to the Hotel Astoria, the more aware I became of the seriousness of my encounter with the major.

Upon reaching the hotel, I had finally sobered up, yet Eric still had limitless enthusiasm and dominated this situation by making me feel, that I was the only woman in the world, to be wanted and loved like this. There was no way to wriggle out of his embrace and protestations of love, and no matter what I tried to say, he dismissed my every excuse. In fact he aroused a passion in me that I did not know existed. As we entered the foyer, my last hope was the staff at the hotel. They would surely prevent him from coming upstairs to my room, or so I thought. But what did I expect at 1 a.m. in the morning? There was only one sleepy old man, sitting by the desk, and he hardly noticed us at all. No-one was going to save me after all, and I dreaded the consequences.

When we reached my room, the scent of the carnations that Protheroe had brought me, filled the air. My suitcases were still standing about, partly unpacked, and only the bed was made. The maid had laid out my light-blue nightie over a cushion. I got Protheroe to sit in the armchair and started talking to him, in an effort to sober him up, but he just ignored me, and slowly began undressing me, kissing my body as the clothes fell to the floor.

We fell into each other's arms with Eric half singing "You do something to me nobody else can do". With that my resistance vanished, in the belief that we were destined for each other . . . . .

Rather touchingly, before he left early the next morning, he tied the little bows on my night-dress and said "I only wish I had the guts to run away with you now, to a place where no-one knows us, but then you are not the type who, could be in love with a deserter." He then kissed me passionately, goodbye. Minutes later my telephone rang, and I guessed who it would be. It was Eric, telling me that he still loved me, and with that he rang off.

The following week was one of sheer bliss, with flowers arriving, accompanied by little coded messages, and telephone calls which set the wires on fire. I truly believed that such happiness could never end. But when Eric called to take me to his new flat on the 'Rupolph von Alt Platz', I guessed that something was wrong.

When we arrived there, unpacked suitcases greeted us. His subdued manner gave me an inclination, of what was in store for me. My fears were soon confirmed, when he said in a hushed tone of voice "My wife will be coming to stay with me, whilst I am working here in Vienna. She is due to arrive tomorrow, so you must be sensible and understand . . . ". He had not finished the words, as I burst into floods of tears, for I already knew the rest. I looked at him in anguish and ran out of the door, as he shouted after me "I'll drive you back to the hotel Darling!" I flew down the steps, as if wild horses were after me. How could I have been so stupid? Now he wanted me to be sensible! Are those really phrases that one can use to substitute a love like we had? I should have guessed, that a handsome man like Protheroe would be married, but I was too much besotted by him, but how could I sit in judgement? If only we both had not been married? Crying openly on the streets, was not a luxury I would normally have allowed myself, but today all was lost. I did not care that passers-by stared at me, as tears fell to the ground and mingled with the leaves on the pavement.

Upon reaching my hotel, in the safety of my room, I suddenly got angry and blamed myself for giving in. The telephone rang and the receptionist told me that Herr Zartl, from the nearby cafe was eager to see me on important business. She asked if she could send him up to me.

"Why not," I nearly answered, "One man more or less will make no difference." But of course I controlled myself and gave a polite "Yes".

Herr Zartl had been an old family friend, whom I had known for many years. He arrived with a big brief-case, which when opened contained thousands of pound notes. I immediately asked him what he wanted me to do with all that money. His reply was swift "You have got connections with the British, and you could exchange the pounds into Austrian schillings. I will give you 10 per cent if you will do this for me."

My eyes rested on all that money now lying on my table, and I asked myself whether this was another nudge of fate, or whether he was simply trying to involve me in something shady. Herr Zartl came from a very distinguished restaurant family and was very wealthy in his own right. Luckily for me, being a man with his own problems, he did not notice my red eyes, but told me how well I looked. This was surely the overstatement of the year I thought, but I asked him, if he wished me to make him some tea. He declined, wanting to get back to his cafe, which was frequented mainly by British troops, who spent a great deal of money playing cards there. The reason he had approached me, was that gambling was strictly forbidden on premises other than gambling houses and those had to have a licence. If he had gone to the bank, with this amount of money to exchange, questions would have been asked. I consequently agreed to help as gambling was not a crime in my book, but said that I wanted to count the money in front of him, so that we would both know how much there was.

I was in the middle of counting when the telephone rang, I motioned to Herr Zartl to answer it.

"A Major Protheroe wishes to speak to you," he said, and I had little choice but to take the call.

In an angry mood, I answered the phone.

"Actually, I was very concerned that you had got back alright, considering the state in which you left here, but I can hear that it hasn't taken you very long to find another man to answer your telephone," came the voice out of the receiver.

If he had been next door, I would have gone round and hit him, but the presence of Herr Zartl calmed me down enough to explain why the latter was in my room, adding that he was also a good friend of the family, and that he was tall, good looking, rich and single. After this I slammed down the receiver, not even waiting for a reply. From the conversation, it was obvious to Herr Zartl that he had come at a rather critical time. He apologised and left, with me promising to see what I could do, with regard to the exchange of his money. At last alone, I called down to reception and instructed them that no further calls were to be put through to my room, as I was resting. It had now dawned on me, that I simply had to rid myself of men, starting with Protheroe, but this aching heart would not stop reminding me of those yesterdays.

The next morning the sun shone, and I decided to visit my relatives. Aunt Jenny believed in serenity, platonic affairs, friendships and emotional security, and told me that I took after my grandmother Louise, who had a life of tempestuous affairs, one of which resulted in my mother's birth. She added that there were probably a few skeletons in the cupboard that had never seen the light of day. Men had simply adored her, and women hated her outright, as she was as good a wife, as she was a mistress, and never gave the men in her lives a dull moment to remember. I wondered whether this would be my destiny as well, and I asked my aunt what her opinion of the matter was.

She replied "Life is what you make it my dear, and even though you seem rather susceptible to short-term love affairs, you are tenacious on matters of principle."

With that advice, I departed in a taxi, returning to the Hotel Astoria, which had now become my sanctuary and playground of further romances, one of which was already waiting mysteriously in the wings.

To cheer myself up, I dressed in an elegant wool two-piece suit, which showed every curve in my body, and went downstairs to dine. With the same intent, a rather expensively dressed gentleman, joined me in the lift. "I am going to have dinner" he said, as if it were a revelation.

I smilingly replied "What a coincidence, so am I."

"So why not join forces?" my unexpected date added with a glint in his light-brown eyes, and we left the lift, his arm already holding mine.

I threw a last glance into the mirror of the lift, assessing my conquest. Indeed, he had a strong face and jawline, but his mouth was rather weak and sensual. Although, this was strictly an officer's transit hotel, he was dressed in a impeccably tailored suit, which enhanced his tall broad figure. We walked into the crowded dining-room towards a centre table, with reserved on it. Fritz, the head waiter hurried over to us, bowed low and said "Herr General-Direktor, you are early tonight."

Did I hear right? Major Protheroe, who the hell do you think you are, I thought to myself, still hurting badly! I concentrated all my charm on the man now sitting opposite me, who was openly examining my face, whilst introducing himself.

"Kornelius de Kuypers, but I served as a major in Indonesia," he said, in a seductive low voice.

I paused for a moment, and then replied "Mrs Ell."

"And?" he enquired bending over towards me.

"Burgi, Herr General-Direktor," I whispered.

"Oh?" he asked twice, as if to make certain he understood my name.

Somehow all the other people in the dining-room faded away, as he reached across the table for my hand and kissed it, saying "Please call me Kor, Mrs Ell, and, I do not need to tell you how lovely, you look tonight."

"Oh, but you do," I retorted emphatically, and we both laughed so loud, that some of the other guests began to stare at us.

The heavy scent of obsession was enfolding Kornelius de Kuypers, like the low-cut two piece, I was wearing, and the stage for romance was set.

By now, I should have known that there was no such thing as the perfect man, as my past errors of judgement weighed heavily on my conscience. But the need to fill a gap in my heart, made me believe in the ultimate dream, of fulfilment. A 'Moonlight Sonata' atmosphere was in the air, or would this turn out to be just another 'Halleluja Chorus', I wondered?

The resident pianist was playing soft music, with my companion unable to take his eyes off me. We established that we had quite a few things in common. De Kuypers was a linguist, fluent in Dutch, French, German and perfect in English. He was thirty-five years old, and within half an hour, I knew his entire family history, and that he was lonely, in Vienna.

"What with all the pretty girls around you, Herr General-Director?" I asked.

He touched my arm and said: "You must easily be the most beautiful woman in this hotel . . . . so why should I look for another . . . . ?"

'Why indeed' thought my ego, but my mind was not quite sure if he was really my type of man. All I could go on for the present, was my instinct, and this was mainly directed by my heart, which was vengeful, and wanted to show Protheroe that there were much bigger fish in the sea, than him.

As it turned out Kornelius De Kuypers soon healed my wounded heart with the loveliest flowers I had ever seen, and expensive perfumes, sent direct from Paris. I was also given the use of his chaffeur-driven car, to take me whenever, and wherever I desired to go, and his love, was in complete contrast to the 'hurricane love' that Protheroe had offered. De Kuypers was a passive force, tactful, well mannered, full of etiquette and gentility; the result of his wealthy, but kind upbringing in Holland.

We agreed to meet every evening for dinner, as he worked during the day as Managing Director at Unilever's factory in Vienna. I waited eagerly for the telephone to ring to tell me that Kor was back. Indeed, a special blend of magic was established between us!

When one afternoon he returned unexpectedly from a board meeting, dashing into my room saying: "It's no use trying to avoid the truth . . . . . I am in love with you Burgi," I was not surprised, as he took me into his arms and kissed me.

My own heart lifted from the turmoil of being rejected by Protheroe, to the miracle of a new love. I did not want Kor to replace Eric, but to erase him from my mind.

The following morning, a bouquet of dark red roses arrived, with a note in an envelope which read: 'Darling Burgi, this time it's love my foolish heart.'

By now, all my remaining doubts had vanished, and I decided to introduce Kor to my illustrious Aunt Jenny, The Baroness von Haan. I expected her strong dissapproval, as she was a staunch Catholic, and I prepared myself for it. But to my utter amazement, she announced that Kor would be the perfect partner for me, a view that was no doubt influenced by the fact that he was the heir, to the famous De Kuypers' liqueur fortune. My still being married to Ell, seemed all of a sudden to be of little importance to her, as she actually said to De Kuypers: "A faint heart, never won a fair lady."

Kor was so smitten with our aristocratic background, plus my relatives made me into a vision of perfection, and as always, I was swept away, on a wave of happiness. Indeed, I had never been one to tiptoe through the tulips, but rather one, that waded right into the fields, promising paradise.

However, the question in my heart still remained . . . . . . had Kor really managed to burn out my passion for Major Protheroe?

By now, it was a foregone conclusion that I would divorce Ell, as De Kuypers had asked me to marry him. He even flew to London to engage a well-known barrister to deal with my divorce.

Every evening at 7 p.m., he would ring, saying: "I love you . . . . do you still love me?" He would then proceed to give me a progress report, how to get my divorce.

Kor, came back from London, loaded with gifts. He also brought back a ring. It had the largest aquamarine stone, in a platinum setting, that I had ever seen. He placed it on my finger saying: "This is forever" and kissed me.

'Forever' was a word I dreaded, as I had heard it too many times before, but I swore to myself, that this time nothing must go wrong.

We then sat down and talked about the future. Not only, had he been to see my solicitor, but also his own, to finalise his divorce from his Swiss-born wife.

I had known from the beginning, that the De Kuypers had been separated five years, and that a divorce was merely a legal technicality, for their solicitors, to sort out a settlement for his wife, and two sons.

This would have been straightforward. Kor, however, had been informed in London that his wife had made an additional stipulation to the settlement, making it plain, that if he really divorced her, he would never be allowed to see his two sons again.

I was horrified at the cruelty of the woman, but Kor, genuinely stated that none of this mattered, and that it was merely a minor hiccup, and that he would agree to her terms, just to get his divorce out of the way.

He told me however, that there was a much bigger obstacle. Under English law, I would not be free, to remarry until I had been separated from my husband, for two complete years. This news nearly floored me, but seemed to have no effect on Kor who said: "No problem is insurmountable. All that matters, is that we are together. We will simply live together, until your divorce comes through, and then we will marry."

In my mind, a big ugly cloud, had moved over my sunny world, and what had seemed at first, as a straightforward parting of the ways, had now become a mountain of debris, the size of Everest to me.

We had already been offered living accommodation in an empty wing of my aunt's house, which should have been an incentive for me to settle down, but I began to have doubts, which of course, I kept strictly to myself.

Was it really fair to ask any man to sacrifice his children for me? More to the point, would he one day resent me for it?

I would of course have to give up my career, and would I really be able to adjust my life, as the beautiful acquisition of a De Kuyper? Could I be happy living in the shadows of the great name of De Kuyper, when my ambitions had only been a few weeks previous, to carve my own name among the famous, through my own talent for singing and acting?

Moreover, did I possess the patience of waiting another two years, and would he truly still want to marry me then?

I had no answers to any of these questions and decided for the moment to go through the motions of preparing myself for a future, that seemed with every minute to become more, and more uncertain.

So my first port of call was Professor Fischer. When I informed him that I was going to give up my career, to live with De Kuypers, he was devastated. He remarked that to give up my singing career was a crime, and that although he admired De Kuypers, he could not see that material things could compensate me for the adulation that an audience would give me. He added, that sooner or later I would regret what I had done with my life, and that I would blame De Kuypers for it. He urged me to remember what Franz Lehar had said, reiterating "You are a born soubrette, you belong on the stage, and no man should stand in your way."

Was he right?

After a lot of soul-searching, I came to the conclusion that De Kuypers and I were not destined for each other. Yet, I felt guilty having to deal such a blow to the man who believed in me, and loved me. However, my courage in the belief that I was doing the best thing for both of us determined me, to see this through to the bitter end. I arranged to meet Kor in a cafe and sat myself in the darkest corner of the room, so that he could not see the tears in my eyes. I explained at great length, why we had to part and offered him his ring back, which he refused. To my astonishment, he removed his gold watch and placed it in front of me, saying "I won't be needing this where I am going, back to the Indonesian battlefields. Apart from this, it will only remind me of the 7 o'clock rendezvous, we shared every evening." With these parting remarks he walked out of the cafe, like a 'lamb going to slaughter'.

I just sat there devastated at what I had done, and at that moment, I wished that I had never been born. My mind was heavy with recriminations, asking myself, what right I had to inflict so much pain, on someone who had offered his all.

The next day I heard through the receptionist that De Kuypers had left the hotel in a hurry, explaining that he had been called back to Holland. This saved me the embarrassment of having to make any kind of excuses. Everything was back to normal . . . or so I thought!

Quite unexpectantly, Kamilla the receptionist made every effort to become friendly, inviting me out to lunch on her days off. As I had nothing better to do, I could see no harm in it, but found from her conversations, that part of her life story, she told me, definitely did not ring true. Always curious, I tried to pinpoint her down on some of the things that made no sense, but her answers were rather evasive.

Apparently, she was the widow of a Polish nobleman, yet she deliberately omitted very carefully, to mention her surname. Added to this, she spoke English like someone, who had learned the language. There was not even the smallest hint of an accent. Yet, when I overheard another Polish gentleman at the hotel, trying to strike up a conversation with her, in her supposedly native language, she bluntly refused to talk in Polish, and replied to him in English. Something fishy, was definitely afoot?

She also told me that she was now engaged to a Lieutenant-Colonel Lermonth, whom I had actually met at the Hotel Sacher. When I mentioned this to her, she immediately confided in me, that his estranged wife was suing him for divorce, citing her as co-respondent. She even showed me a document from a court in Edinburgh. She seemed so distraught that I sympathised with her, more out of politeness, than genuine concern. She however, mistook my sympathy as something that we had in common, namely men that treated us badly. There was a bitterness within the woman, that I had not realised existed, as she gave me a run-down, of every man, she had ever come across.

Eager to find out the truth behind this obvious charade, I implied a certain amount of empathy with her, especially in the light of the De Kuyper's affair, which she had understood, to have been the work of just another callous man, ridding himself, of what had become inconvenient.

I allowed her to believe just that, which made her confide in me even further, as she said: "I don't know how I am going to survive, if that wife of his doesn't divorce him, the sword of Damocles is hanging over my head, and if it hadn't been for Lermonth who believed in me, I would have been found out long ago, and put in jail."

I of course replied that surely nothing could be quite that bad, which immediately opened a floodgate to what can only be described as the largest skeleton, that I had ever come across in anyone's cupboard.

She produced a box, and removed from it, a picture album, which she handed me. When I opened it, I got the biggest shock of my life. They were photographs of her in an SS uniform, standing arm in arm with an SS colonel. My eyes nearly dropped out of my head, as she explained to me that his name was Wolff, and that he had deserted her, during the last stages of the war, to face the fury of the Polish people on her own. I had to hold my breath, as she further confided that this Wolff, however, before leaving her, had murdered a Polish officer's wife, so that she could have a passport!

My stomach turned over, and I felt sick, as she continued to rant and rave about how fickle men were, and how the country would have been far better off, if Hitler had managed to create his Arian race.

The thought, that I was sitting opposite a murderess, or at the very least across, an accomplice to murder, made me gather my shattered wits. I remained cool, and agreed and nodded in the right places, and after two hours or so, invented an excuse to leave.

Before returning to my room, I made an appointment at once to see the manager of the hotel, a Captain Spreckley. He was a stockily-built man, with a reddish face, twinkling blue eyes, and a soft voice. He was extremely polite, waiting for me to be seated, before he did the same.

"You are Mrs Ell," he said, "I've seen you often, but always on the arm of a handsome officer, or lately of course, with Major De

Kuypers, one of our VIP guests.''

"Yes, that is correct, but I have not come here to discuss my love life with you, but to make you aware of a discovery of great importance, that has obviously escaped your notice . . . . . namely, that you are employing a possible war criminal, and a woman who is being cited in a divorce case, as co-respondent.'' Captain Spreckley went pale, and asked me, if I had any proof to substantiate such allegations.

So I opened my handbag and gave him the photo of Kamilla in an SS uniform, that I had removed from the album, without her noticing.

Spreckley visibly shrank into his chair.

"Well what are you going to do?" I asked impatiently.

He jumped to his feet and replied: "We'll go to Kamilla's room and sort this out, there must be some mistake." We marched to her room and entered without knocking. Spreckley, with the photo in his hand, confronted the woman, with what I had told him. Her eyes flashed, and before I knew what was happening, she held me by the throat. Spreckley, immediately intervened, throwing her across the room, where she landed on the floor and lay there like a viper, spitting insults at both of us, as only someone from the lowest strata of society would resort to.

She threatened me, and accused him of rape, at the same time, taunting him about his war-damaged face.

All he could do, was order her out of the hotel immediately.

Exhausted, by this fracas, Spreckley ushered me out of the room, and invited me for a drink in his suite. There we discussed the matter at some length, but he dismissed my requests, to have Kamilla placed in the hands of the police.

"Why ever not?" I urged.

So he explained. "It's like this, once the police are called in, they will not only investigate this incident, but, they may start probing into all kinds of activities. As manager of this hotel, I know that there are quite a few skeletons in the cupboard, that had better remain at rest . . " and he added, "I am also a good friend of Colonel Lermonth and if it came to light, his girl-friend was a Nazi, what do you think would happen to his career in the Army?"

Captain Spreckley was pacing up and down in his agitation and anger, with me, demanding justice and retribution, as I suggested various ways and means of dealing with this explosive situation. By now it was patently obvious to me, that he had not the slightest intention of implicating, either the hotel, or himself, and all my pleas fell on deaf ears.

As further arguments on his behalf, he stated that he was related

K

to Air Vice-Marshall Sir Herbert Spreckley, thus such a scandal had to be avoided at all cost. I could not believe what I heard, Kamilla remained scot-free, because the British manager of the Hotel Astoria, was afraid to expose her.

My mind was in a spin and I was wondering . . . did at some stage he really try and have sex with her . . . or even rape her? as she said; and I left his suite extremely disillusioned and went to my room.

I telephoned Professor Fischer and told him of what happened and to my surprise he expressed his own doubts about Kamilla, whom he had met on several occasions, and he said: "Perhaps Captain Spreckley may have fancied her, when he was drunk, but as for myself . . . I should swim for my life, if she had chased me."

Fischer, who was a fierce anti-Nazi, who saw his wife shot by the SS in the last days of fighting in Vienna, had every right to feel indignant at the negative attitude of Captain Spreckley, and he urged me, to inform the Russians of Kamilla and her war crimes. Indeed, I had the strong feeling, that everyone wanted ME to take a firm action and the possible risk of being attacked by one of Kamilla's Nazi thugs. My final appeal was to my aristocratic Aunt Jenny, who in turn blamed Captain Spreckley's weakness, in dealing with this serious matter and she cleverly advised me, to leave it to the gods and put my energy into my new show 'Maske in Blau'.

The following day, I was told by one of the hotel staff, that Kamilla had simply moved out, with no forwarding address of course. Good riddance and shame on Spreckley, was all I could think of for a moment.

Rehearsals for the 'Maske in Blau' began and as usual, I came home very tired, and all I desired was a relaxing bath and go to bed, when I noticed on my little table a brown envelope stamped; His Majesty's Service. A premonition of unwelcome news came over me, as I opened the letter and read;

Dear Madam,
You are requested to contact Major E. Protheroe at the British Embassy, 3, Reisnerstrasse, Room Number 5, to collect your British Passport, which will enable you, to join your husband in the United Kingdom.
Yours faithfully,
E. Protheroe.

A surge of despair went through my body, at the prospect of having to face the major again. I put the evil day off for as long as I could, and finally decided a week later to go and see him.

It was now October, and already there was a chill in the air, with the beckoning of winter. My appointment was for 10 o'clock which gave me plenty of time to prepare myself, for this 'command performance'.

My only thought was to get a signature on my extension papers, no matter what the cost. I firmly believed that the flame inside me for Major Protheroe had been extinguished, so no matter what happened, he would never be able to hurt me again.

However, with his reaction at our first meeting still clearly in mind, I dressed to kill. I wore a tailored black two-piece suit, embossed with silky braided lapels and pockets. Instead of a blouse, I wore a pale-lilac chiffon scarf, which acted as no more than a netted veil, covering my assets. With this, I wore the most outrageous hat, whose netting of tiny dots draped over my face, and fastened to the hat was an exquisite *diamanté* clip.

I took a taxi, but when I walked up the steps of the Consulate, I could not help but remember the ecstasy of our brief, but wild love affair. I was glad to find, on entering Room 5, that there were already several women there; thinking that I would not have to face him all alone.

I sat down to await my turn, and exchanged some idle chatter with some of the ladies, who were all too eager to get to England, as fast as possible. I certainly began to feel like the odd one out, as I had no wish to go to England, but merely wanted an extension to my stay in Vienna.

Suddenly, the door opened and Major Protheroe faced me head on! He looked startled, but said: "Mrs Ell, will you please come in." This produced a murmur of protest, but I took no notice, and swished past him into the office. He shut the door, walked over to his desk and told me to be seated. Before I could do so, he lifted my veil, bent his head close to mine and said: "You're still as lovely as ever." To my own astonishment, he asked me: "How many heads have you turned since we last met?"

I kept my cool and replied: "Isn't your wife woman enough, to satisfy you still?"

As if scalded with hot water, he retreated to the other side of the desk and sat down. He then asked me in a formal tone of voice: "When are you planning to go to England?"

In an equally formal manner, I explained that I had no definite plans yet, as I had received an offer to play the lead in the 'Maske in Blau'.

He immediately congratulated me, adding: "You certainly have come a long way since we last met."

I smiled wickedly at him, and put my gloved hand across the

table saying: "It was probably all for the best, that things happened they way they did — as without your help last time, I probably would not be here today."

To my surprise, he removed my glove, and kissed the palm of my hand, saying: "You little devil you, you're doing it again, twisting me round your little finger."

There was no answer to that, so I gave him a deep smouldering look, followed by my most charming smile. This finally then did the trick. With trembling hands, he released my palm and signed my extension papers for another six months. He pointed out however, that I could no longer stay at the Hotel Astoria, at the expense of the British military, but that I would have to find alternative accommodation, as soon as possible.

Mercifully, he brought our appointment to an end, by handing me my papers saying: "If there is anything else I can do for you, I hope you will not hesitate to call me."

I got to my feet, put my veil back over my face, and put the papers into my handbag.

He too, got up and stood so close to me, that for a few seconds I thought, that he intended kissing me, but instead he asked: "Who are you going to bedazzle now?"

I almost replied "Wouldn't you like to know" but smiled sweetly, and swished past him and out of the building, in the same way that I had arrived.

As soon as I reached the street downstairs, I decided to walk back, in order to think. There was no better place than by walking through the lovely gardens, which led into the park. The colourful leaves underfoot were reminding me of a Persian carpet, as my mind escaped into a world of day-dreams.

The idea of finding lodgings in 1947 in Vienna, was a little like looking and finding a needle in a haystack. I could of course go back to live with my aunt and cousins in the 18th district, but this alone would have created another nightmare, namely that of travelling to and from work, which was in the 3rd district. On top of that, I had no intention of giving up my independence. There was no getting away from it, the Astoria Hotel was not only ideal in that up to now, it had not cost me a penny, but that it afforded me a comfortable life-style, that I simply could not pay for. By the time I returned there, a plan was beginning to formulate in my head, of how I could manage to stay on at the hotel.

I had been aware for some time now, that the manager, Captain Spreckley, looked at me, with more than just formal civility, and I felt sure, that with a little encouragement, I could bring him, under my spell.

The plan was this: Captain Spreckley, was a stickler for punctuality, and always left his suite at 7 p.m., to go down and greet the guests. His suite, just happened to be on my floor. I had to get past it to go to the communal bathrooms, as my own room had only a wash-basin. So, I decided to put on my beautiful flame-red dressing-gown, which Mrs Klima had made for me out of parachute silk. I wore nothing underneath and had a towel over my arm, as I floated down the corridor at exactly 7 p.m.

His doors opened, and there stood my unsuspecting captain, in dress uniform. I immediately apologised for my lack of attire, and bashfully tried to cover my see-through dressing-gown, with the towel.

I rushed into the bathroom leaving the manager dumbfounded in his doorway and listened behind the door for him to descend the staircase, and then I rushed back to my room triumphantly! I got dressed for dinner in a cocktail-dress made of the same material, silk, which was lined, to attract his attention, which I felt would enhance my chances of staying on at this hotel indefinitely.

I went down to dinner, and within minutes was approached by Spreckley, who asked me very humbly, if he could join me. I gracefully agreed, in the happy knowledge, that my plan was working well.

Over dinner, Captain Spreckley came straight to the point, declaring: "Please forgive me for saying this, but you have burned me to cinders, I don't know, how I managed to walk down the stairs and remain dignified, with that vision of you, clouding my entire mind." With that remark, he reached for both my hands across the table, and added: "You have taken away all my senses, Mrs Ell, and my credibility!"

I played the utterly astonished demure little lady, saying: "I am so terribly sorry for any embarrassment, I may have caused. I never realised that I would have such an effect on someone, as powerful as yourself."

"What do you mean by powerful?" he asked, rather intrigued.

"Well simply, that your word is law at this hotel, and I would hate to think, that perhaps you might not be able to help me in my present predicament."

I could see his stature growing by the moment. It was important for me to get Spreckley not only on my side, but to also act as my protector, should Protheroe decide, to enforce his ruling, on my leaving. I knew full well that Spreckley would never ask me to leave the hotel now my womanly instinct told me, that he had surrendered to my charm.

"Oh no dear lady, the fault lay entirely with me, for what man including myself, would not be aware of your sex appeal and your beauty and be seduced by you."

My charm had obviously worked, but what amazed me, was the speed with which I had managed to attain my goal. So I decided to go for broke explaining that he was very generous not to have taken offence, as I would have hated to have left under such unhappy circumstances.

"What is all this talk about leaving?" he enquired, and so I told him of the delicate position, I found myself in, adding that Major Protheroe had given me his orders this very day.

To which Captain Spreckley forcefully replied: "I am the manager of this hotel and I decide who stays and who goes." His broad and trembling hand reached across for mine and he said: "Let me assure you Mrs Ell, you are staying."

As if surprised, I replied: "Oh you are so masterful, indeed you are just what I need, a strong man to guide me."

Captain Spreckley came closer, his eyes flickered nervously and he said: "It all depends on the prize. Sometimes, it's worth everything Mrs Ell. I may be risking my rank for you."

"I don't . . . I don't understand," I answered coyly, as his powerfully built body pressed against me and he whispered in my ear: "Of course, I want to make love to you. Am I crazy, to say such a thing?"

He was crazy at this moment of blatant desire, but I dare not tell him that; but I let his eyes stray over my curvacious body and he declared in a low voice: "Let's drop the formality and call me Michael; we have already crossed the line between friends and lovers."

I smiled at the thought, of how easy it was to seduce this man, who was completely under my spell, disintegrating like a snowflake kissed by the sun.

Fritz, the head waiter, came over and winked knowingly at me, making a little well-known joke in German; "Ich bleib' dir treu, von drei bis vier". Which means, I'll be faithful from 3 p.m. — 4 p.m., and Michael looked rather curiously at both of us.

I ridiculed the waiter and told Captain Spreckley, that it was simply a joke in poor taste, and I called Fritz a veritable terror and we dismissed him by giving him our orders for dinner.

After the meal, which was excellent, and a feast to me, we sat and sipped champagne as we listened to the pianist Professor Bauer, who played my favourite melody, "Wenn der weisse Flieder wieder blueht komm und kuess ich deine Lippen mued" (When the white lilac blooms again, I shall come and kiss your lips again.)

Upon leaving the luxurious dining-room arm in arm, under the envious looks of his fellow officers, Michael beamed happily, as if to flaunt his authority and he kept telling me, to keep smiling. On our way out, he also complimented the pianist, on his rendering of the White Lilac song and he instructed him, to play it every time I entered the restaurant. "Satisfied, Darling?" he asked.

Michael escorted me to my room and I wondered, what thoughts were going through his mind? There was no instant willingness on my part to ask him in, although as he pointed out at dinner; he wanted to know all about my life.

"All?" I enquired teasingly. "You may be shocked, to put it mildly." But his reply was a kiss on my cheek.

We paused at my bedroom door and his slightly hooded blue eyes skimmed across my face; his voice rather sophisticated aloof — "I've loved every minute, of being with you this evening Burgi, in particular your at times, mischievous humour" and he pulled me towards his trembling body and said: "May I call on you tomorrow, I simply could not function without you now?"

My brain told me that it was dangerous to get involved with this man, yet it was also exhilarating, because my strength matched his, or so my cold appraisal told me, and I could not quite believe my luck, everything I wanted had dropped into my lap; almost too good to be true.

How did my song go, which I had sung recently on stage? 'I have known love that was bitter sweet . . I have known passion . . I've known retreat . . I have explored all the channels of bliss . . and I have tasted . . never wasted one kiss.'

Suddenly, my instincts told me, this Captain Spreckley was not like the other men who had wanted me; easily dismissed, he spelt danger. I really could not afford a confrontation. His last kiss demanded response from me, whilst I froze regaining control over my body, yet I asked myself; am I to scorn this opportunity of staying in my beloved Vienna?

My efficient other self, demanded proof of his powers, as the manager of this five-star Hotel Astoria, whilst under British occupation.

I did not have to wait long, indeed the very next morning, two porters arrived with instructions, to move me bag and baggage into a fabulous suite, opposite Captain Spreckley's. Instead of moving out, I was moving up in the world, into an apartment reserved for VIPs.

Michael received me in style with beautiful dark-red roses and a generous smile, plus a profound statement; or question? "Are you the lady, my lonely heart so often imagined, or just a cold and lovely creation?" He took me into his arms and kissed me and I knew, that it would take every ounce of my acting to contain the flames that soared through his forty-two-year-old body.

The long-stemmed roses fell to the floor, and with my eyes closed, I told Michael that I will make him happy and remain loyal.

"That's all I wanted to hear my darling; my love is strong enough, for the two of us."

I had a good look at Michael's face, it certainly had strength, and the awful injury to his nose, caused by an explosion in his tank was obvious, and he pointed to it and said: "You must never refer to it, or pity me Burgi, or ask questions about how it happened. I want to forget the war and live a normal life with you. Is that clearly understood?"

Tears were running down my face, to think, he lost his wife, the mother of his four children and was badly injured into the bargain. So how could I have the audacity to hurt him any more? I always seemed in a war of heart and mind, at one moment hopeful, the next despairing and apprehensive, and turmoil went through my body as once more I was caught in a web I created myself, encouraging desires by manipulation. Yet it was too dangerous to reveal that inner soft part, my heart. What followed reads like a Cinderella story, with Michael catering to my every wish, and suddenly, I was able to indulge in an existence of sheer luxury, with him giving me all his ration, cigarettes, bottles of whisky, to sell on the black market at the highest prices. In return, I was able to engage my own dress designer, a Frau Klima, who once worked for the famous Dior in Paris and it was she, who made me fully aware of my figure and colouring, and how to use and enhance these assets.

Michael was by now totally captivated and agreed with whatever I did and he found fulfilment in my company of make-believe. Perhaps fate had chosen me to bring a little happiness, into his rather dull life and I could see nothing wrong, in promoting my various enterprises, with Captain Spreckley's blessing.

Before long, he asked me to marry him, after my divorce, which was pending and to prove how serious his intentions were, he telephoned his brother, Air Vice-Marshal Sir Herbert Spreckley, in my presence, telling him that I was his special girl and the niece of Baroness Haan.

"Are wedding bells in order, dear Michael?" I heard Sir Herbert say.

"Time will tell, but we are so happy Herbert, so very happy," and he gave me the receiver to add a few words and I wished him and his family a prosperous 1948, and the air vice-marshal replied;

"Bless you for looking after our Michael, my dear; he's a splendid fellow."

With mixed feelings, I hung up and we continued to celebrate the last few hours of 1947, in an atmosphere of abandoning all reason, as the champagne flowed like water. There I lay in the arms of Michael, who loved and adored me in an agony of self-recrimination, wiping away the wantonness, as though I had never existed, and I pulled myself away, straightening the material of my dress.

Michael expected explosive chemistry, thundering out of control, yet his words trailed into silence, concealing my feelings, to its cool logic.

The first week of 1948 began rather hectic, not only had I established myself as the 'first lady' at Hotel Astoria, I was also cast for the lavish production of the lead in a big revue named 'Maske in Blau'. The part suited me to perfection, a beautiful actress playing with fire, which in the end boomeranged on her. Additionally, I had been kept in the wings for 'The Merry Widow' with the great and most handsome leading man in Vienna, Fred Liewehr, as Danilo; so WHO could possibly have asked for anything more? Surrounded by adulation, passionately wooed by Captain Spreckley, who had to content himself with kisses only, plus my for him exclusive 'fashion displays', which rendered him in a state of delight, I managed to enjoy my life to the hilt. My noble cousins, plus my dear Aunt Jenny, who basically was a puritan, approved of what I was doing, because I was 'clever' enough, as they put it, to keep all men at bay, but dangling from my little finger, and in constant attendance, at the sight of my frivolous hats. It was now, or never for me, to reach my goal, as mainly a singer and as a society hostess and to be seen at the right places. The most important and rich people sought me out and Professor Fischer, who was not only a great music and singing teacher, but also my confidant, introduced me to his millionaire son-in-law Dipl. Ing. Haberhauser, who offered me a partnership in his newly-formed company. One of his partners was the brother of Dr Kissinger and although they had the money, I had the British contacts to buy what was needed; army lorries, sold off near Klagenfurt. I consulted Michael and we all met and he agreed to let us use, my old room, as an 'office', and I engaged a private secretary, after interviewing a string of girls.

My aunt was flabbergasted at my energy and enterprise, not only was I in demand on stage, but also the executive of a transport company, operating from the British Hotel Astoria. "Whatever next will Burgi think of?'' she exclaimed to her daughter and friends. Indeed, for much longer, I asked myself?

Somehow, I convinced Michael, that he was the 'Caesar' of all he surveyed and the sheer audacity, with which I tackled VIPs, including General Mark Clark and the French general, whose wife became my best friend, thus persuading her husband to close if not both eyes, one, to the goings on, and support my schemes. I organised the most splendid parties at my aunt's mansion; hired small bands and students, who dressed in gold livery to wait on my illustrious friends and cater to their whims. Of course, I always had to contribute my own talent, by singing songs, they requested, creating enchantment and delight amongst the guests. *"Liebe du Himmel auf Erden . . ewig besteh''* — "Love you heaven on earth, rule forever," I sang, and they asked for more . . . heaven . . . or should it mean money, to buy their heaven. In those turbulent days, nearly everything and everyone was for sale; in particular love and for so little — a packet of cigarettes, a tin of sardines — how awful I thought. I who had no more need to seek out suitable business as clients, they came and coveted me, in order to do business and make extra money. My name alone secured an invitation to the best parties, with Captain Spreckley supporting all my extraordinary enterprises, and I often marvelled at his daring in obeying the rules as the manager of this transit hotel.

At one time, Michael was the best man at a colonel's wedding, and the girl was like me; half Czech, twenty-five, blonde and beautiful, but homeless and poor. She married a much older British officer to obtain food for herself and her parents. I was the guest of honour and my dress designer made an extra effort to create a fabulous ensemble in silver-grey georgette. It was a two piece, three-quarter length, embossed with orchids at the bottom of the slim skirt, and on the very wide sleeves. Frau Klima nearly poured me into this outfit and pinned a dark-red rose on the left side, whilst my hat had another silk rose on the top right, to accentuate its ultra elegance.

When Michael and I arrived at the church, all heads turned and the ah's could be clearly heard rumbling through the congregation. Flash bulbs went off and I smiled, with tears in my throat, when I saw the lovely bride in a white silk gown kneeling down taking the oath of obedience in English 'I obey and forsake all others . .' her clear voice stated. I looked at Michael who stood next to the groom, tall and proud, and I wondered, what was going on in his mind. God give me the strength, I prayed for the first time in many weeks, to be honest with myself to withstand the physical demands of Spreckley and tears began running down my face and I realised people were watching me; Melanie for one, who knew me well. I was glad when the ceremony was over and I could mingle with the bride and groom, and their embraces hid my sadness, yet everyone complimented me on my stunning outfit as usual. We proceeded to the Hotel Sacher, where the reception was being held in absolute splendour. Yet again, I seemed to be the centre of attraction, with Eva hugging me and crying, whilst her new husband began drinking with Michael. Eva and I had so much in common; we both married because we were hungry; we both fought the Nazis and received three cheers, and she recalled our carefree days at the convent, when I knocked off the head of Joseph, playing handball and told them to glue it together with Uhu; and when I put pyjama buttons into the little "nigger boy" to save our money to buy ice-creams and was punished with solitary confinement for one week; and when they collected food for me and placed the sandwiches into the organ pipes, which at the morning service were out of order, until Sister Rosa discovered the 'reason' or better, the faulty parts, mainly some surplus bread, distorting the sound of the organ! Those were the days of frolics and laughter, now she was Mrs Hawkins and I was Mrs Ell and both of us British subjects, with responsibilities.

After the wedding breakfast, a small band played dance music and to my utter amazement, Colonel Hawkins got hold of me to dance. He was slightly intoxicated and he said; "I think, I've married the wrong girl." What bad taste, I thought but smiled silently and wriggled out from his arms and into Michael's, who obviously realised the '*faux pas*' of his friend, dancing with me and not his bride of a few hours.

From now on, I counted the minutes, for the wedding festivities to come to an end, and when Eva asked me to accompany her upstairs, helping her with the change of clothing, I obliged.

Once alone, she broke down and cried, expressing doubts, that she had made a mistake, after all Gordon was much older and known for his heavy drinking. Was she able to change his habits?

"Of course, he loves you Eva," I assured her, as she discarded her wedding gown and hung it in the wardrobe.

Then, to my surprise, she put on a grey anorak and a black cap, like mine and which we wore in the Resistance and she said with a tear trailing down her blonde locks; "Burgi, that is how I want *you* to remember me, should this be our last farewell."

I nearly broke down myself, swallowing my tears and promising to recall this moment forever, and we embraced and kissed, then stood back and smartly saluted each other, and I exclaimed; "Long live Austria and Freedom."

Was this the end of a near perfect day, the end of a friendship, and was I destined to marry again, and become Mrs Michael Spreckley?

Time alone will tell, and life at the 'Astoria' continued and we enjoyed every moment of it, as if it was going to be our last; indeed perhaps Michael looking at himself in the mirror, every day he shaved, may have decided, that we all owed him a debt, of being disfigured for life, on behalf of liberty. *I* for one accepted it, seeing my best friends tortured, in the chambers of the Gestapo and I encouraged him, to take what the army had to offer, and we became rather arrogant in demanding the ultimate!

The servants in those far-off days were truly humble, just to have something to eat, reduced them to near slaves, bowing and kissing hands in the old Austrian fashion; and when I handed out my unwanted clothing, they scrambled to get into line first. However, my personal woman servant, Maria came close to being reverent, and I had to stop her treating me like a queen, as I felt guilty of using my exalted circumstances to put her down, although, I knew her husband was a former member of the Nazi party, and revelled in giving the Hitler salute.

The staff of the Hotel Astoria consisted only of Austrian citizens, some of those having served for many years before the British had taken it over, and one in particular, was the head waiter Fritz, tall and angular, with protruding brown eyes, which tried to hypnotize you, if you let them? Fritz fancied himself as a great inventor and bombarded Captain Spreckley and I, with his weird contraptions, yet we listened and watched intently, while he unfolded in stages like a rabbit from a hat, his glorious gadgets! We really did not mind, applauding his genius, if he used the proper time to reveal it, but Fritz came at *all* times, knocking at the door and producing his wizardry, provocatively demonstrating how his contraptions worked. One day he insisted (after all it was only early 1948), the steam iron, bringing one along, which steamed out the entire suite! Michael and I laughed so much, that it hurt, and we nearly needed a doctor to unravel our muscles. There was no end to Fritz, the inventor, he promised to take us into his confidence and partnership if we so wished, and make us rich beyond all dreams.

Perhaps, luckily for me, Fritz saved me from the increasing demands of Michael to share his bed, because it was him, who brought Captain Spreckley's sumptuous breakfast on a trolley, and always shouted outside the suite; "Breakfast for ONE or TWO, Sir?"

Indeed, that stopped Michael from 'producing' me in the early morning, or cancelling the usual timetable for his eating habits in the hotel; adding to this fact, the late hours we kept with entertaining, Michael needed all his energy, to cope with the functioning of this large establishment.

Finally, to stop any possible intimacy, I always dressed to perfection, and was in the company of my two cousins, who arrived at any time, having a free smoke and drink, so generously offered and supplied by my admirer, or fiance, as he called himself, when we were alone.

However, I had to be on guard, for Michael threatened more than once to shoot me if I deceived him, or played around with other men; thus the greatest of care was needed, as he had eyes everywhere. Only on stage and in rehearsals, was I able to imagine the ecstasy of loving and feeling the flames licking my body, to make me aware that I was a young and beautiful woman, romantic and sensitive, who wanted to be kissed and feel the masculine arms and closeness of a man; to hear the erratic beat of his heart, and drowning in the sensation, of fulfilment and love.

Yes, there were plenty of men around me, glancing at me with that certain look of invitation, erotic and teasingly; but the fears of being caught out by Michael made me afraid and fearful of every encounter, with any other officer, and adopt a mask of aloofness.

I had enough irons in the fire already, without adding to my array of business ventures, but I did not have the heart to turn him down outright, merely postponing the evil day!

Perhaps, the funniest of Fritz's so-called immortal inventions was "der schäumende Schwamm". The words alone sent Captain Spreckley into hysterics! This was a sponge filled with liquid soap, which was supposed to last many months.

"When next you have a bath Madam, I will demonstrate it to you," he exclaimed.

From then on I locked my bathroom, in case he really tried this 'Schwamm' out on me!

Michael and I were now caught in a spiral of events, from which there was no escape, with visitors to the hotel increasing by the hour, who had absolutely nothing to do, with the military. By rights, they should not really have stayed there, as this was strictly a British Officers' Transit Hotel! We could both only hope, that the balloon would not go up, and that no-one would report the activities, to London.

My twenty-fifth birthday was near, and I decided to celebrate it at my aunt's house. Spreckley agreed that we should do it in style and made all the arrangements. As it was very cold in January, he ordered for coal to be taken to the Haan's mansion, plus plenty of food, which was prepared at the hotel.

Frau Klima, who was now more my friend than my dressmaker, had a surprise for me, which of course Michael had ordered, and paid for. It was a stunning black satin lace night-gown and negligee, with the smallest pink bows, I had ever seen. I remarked that midgets must have made them!

She insisted that I tried it on and said: "Looking at you from that angle, with your white shimmering skin, just visible through the lace, I can understand why the captain is like a moth, burned up by a flame" and she added "Poor Michael is nearly old enough to be your father, please be kind to him!"

This comment made me think, but how was I to tell what the future held for us? Perhaps even, time was standing still? I often had the notion that here in Vienna I was living in an ivory tower enjoying adulation, but not actually moving forwards, or backwards. I often wondered how I survived this far, but the only answer was, by being, what God made me!

I had been thrown at the tender age of sixteen into a horrific war, yet, by the good fortune of my looks and the cunning use of them, I had outlived the nine lives of a cat. This was mainly because, I had attracted the attention, or more to the point, the readiness, of men to exploit women. But what most of them had not realised is, that I had used this for my own purposes. I had made up my mind, that the one-man woman, only existed in fairy-tales. However, I still tried hard to aspire to those dreams, if only I could fall in love forever with one man, this would have been my ultimate wish, if a fairy godmother had asked me.

Only my cousin Mitzi, was able to see straight through my pretence of loving Captain Spreckley, and she made up a little rhyme about him: "What I wanted . . . . . Michael granted".

She was perfectly right, this really summed up the total content of our relationship. Indeed, he was the keeper of Aladdin's lamp; my every wish just waiting to be expressed, would come true. My passion for beautiful clothes, hats and accessories became a reality and my couture became the 'talk' of Vienna! Frau Klima, inspired by the offers of 'black market food', whisky and cigarettes, managed to get me the most dazzling fabrics, and draped them over me like Joseph's multi-coloured dreamcoat. Captain Spreckley was bewitched and bewildered, but said 'yes' to my every whim, no matter what the cost. Frau Klima created and Michael admired! One particular favourite was a printed crêpe evening-gown, with a plunging backline, which was emphasised with a black velvet bow. It rather shocked my aunt, but I decided to wear it anyway, to please Michael at my twenty-fifth birthday party, on the 21st January in 1948.

The guest list was impressive. There was a French general, who came with his very beautiful wife, and her twenty-two-inch waist; even though she was the mother of two teenage boys, caused quite a stir. My aunt, for the first time since the war ended, showed off her still very presentable figure and status, as a relative of the Royal Habsburg family, by wearing a silver-grey crêpe de Chine gown, which she adorned with her beloved pearl necklace. In fact everyone who came, from princes to baronets all looked perfectly splendid; except for my cousin Nelly, who as usual let the side down, by appearing in a practical pinafore dress with a ghastly blouse to match.

It was 'THE PARTY' and probably will be talked about for many years to come. Expensive flowers arrived all day long; but the most beautiful arrangement came from Michael — it was a white lilac tree in full bloom. To top it all, two of his staff brought a huge chocolate cake, which was decorated with white water-lilies, scattered on the surface, and inscribed 'Happy Birthday Darling'. Even my most exclusive friends had not seen such artistry on a cake before. Michael and I were the centre of attention, being congratulated, and lifted into orbit, beyond our wildest dreams.

The usually sober Professor Fischer danced and flirted openly with a lady called Suzanne, when, suddenly, her husband erupted and threatened to shoot the poor professor. Michael and another colonel had to restore order, whilst Suzanne's husband, pulled her outside, and neither was seen or heard of again.

From that moment on, the party was doomed, and slowly the other guests departed, their fun having, been somewhat spoiled. Michael was the only one to stay. He too was infuriated with the French pair, but remarked that my birthday had nevertheless been a great occasion, one that would not be forgotten easily.

As the weeks passed, Captain Spreckley was now convinced that I was the only woman for him, despite the rife rumours in the hotel that he was consorting with a married lady. Several of the guests began to use this term loosely, but there was nothing anyone could do about wagging tongues, so I simply stood by him, to give him at least, moral support.

When some time later, I had an offer to stay with some friends, I decided to move out of the Hotel Astoria, as the rumours had turned into everyday gossip, with people pointing fingers.

Dr Heinrich Mueller was an eminent judge, and his wife Hansi was very sweet. As they could see no wrong in my liaison with Captain Spreckley, I moved in with them, in the hope of thus, salvaging something of his reputation.

Not long after my birthday, Captain Spreckley handed in his resignation, storming out as a matter of pride, but not before throwing down the gauntlet, by exposing several affairs, that he knew about, between women officers, some of them married, and men staying at the hotel. This may not have been the act of a gentleman, as he remarked, but why should he get the treatment of the 'black sheep', whilst the others disguised themselves in a cloak of respectability, that really wasn't theirs to wear.

Michael had been right to a point, but had he not gone too far, on an issue that needed discretion, when in the case of 'Kamilla', which had cried out for action, he had completely dodged the issue.

However, all was not lost; shortly after this incident, he was promoted to major and posted as manager at the Grand Hotel in Bruck, some 150km from Vienna. He asked me to come with him, but I declined, as I was close to appearing in the revue of 'Maske in Blau'; besides that, it gave me a breathing space, as I was truly not sure, if I really wanted commitment on the scale, that Michael was suggesting.

He did, however come to the final rehearsal, and when Herr Mayerhofer sang: *"Schau einer schönen Frau nie zu tief in die Augen . . . sie sieht den nächsten Mann genau so zärtlich an. Lass dir das eine Warnung sein . . . und dich auf garnichts ein . . . denn eine schöne Frau . . gehört dir nie allein."* — "Don't look too deep into the eyes of a beautiful woman . . . she looks just as tenderly at the next man. Let it be your warning, and don't let yourself in for anything . . . as a beautiful woman never totally belongs to you alone."

This warning came far too late for poor Michael, and I began to feel guilty. We still saw each other on his days off, travelling to and from Vienna to see shows, like 'Die Frau des Potiphar'. It was a biblical play about adultery; Major Spreckley must have sensed that we were growing apart, and remarked after the show: "I truly believe, that we pay for all the happiness we have in life with tears, yet my most happy time I have spent with you. Please, if you ever think of cheating on me, make sure that I'll never catch you . . . . or I would kill you."

A cold shudder went through my body, for I knew that Michael meant what he said! I made up my mind, that this would be the last time, that I ever played with love, a love that had its tender moments, but in which my heart was not really committed.

A new chapter of my life was about to unfold, and punish me for all the things I had done selfishly, in attempt to reach the ultimate, both in my career and also in my private life.

I had created a woman that did not exist, pointing my compass north, south and west, pretending to be tough, whilst really I was vulnerable.

There were hundreds of girls in my position, who came from ordinary homes and had just the most basic in education. One would have thought, that with the advantages I had, educated in the best of schools, brought up by a family full of tradition, mingled with the Royal blood of the Habsburgs, with a talent for acting and singing, success would be a foregone conclusion, but not so.

If one even just considered my potential as a human being, I was no stick in the mud, I overheard a conversation between two British officers at my aunt's house, one trying to dissuade the other from getting involved with me saying: "Stay clear of Burgi, you would not last five minutes with her."

His friend's reply was short but sweet: "But just think of those five minutes, old boy . . ."

But none of this, was to be any help to me now, as fate had turned her back on me. No matter how hard I tried, I could not get a contract with the 'Volkstheatre' because I was a British subject. Only out of work Austrian singers were considered. How paradoxical??? I strived to achieve fame, in my own country but was rejected by the Vanquished. Rather sadly, the only one pleased about this was Major Spreckley, and he wrote to me, saying that maybe now we could settle down and grow old together.

The very thought made me shiver, as he was already twenty years my senior. There was only one thing left to do, and that was to pack my extensive wardrobe and head for England, where I needed to sort out my divorce, and maybe start a new life, as I was now treated as a foreigner by my own people.

I packed my designer hats, with feathers in all directions. Then I started on my suitcases and memories flooded back as I placed the various outfits into the cases. Every ensemble held a secret, an affair, or a magic moment, that would never, and could never, be erased from my memory.

There was, my rather limited, but ultra chic Protheroe wardrobe, reminding me of an affair that could have qualified for the Olympic sprint. Then I packed away an impressive range of clothes that marked the Spreckley-period.

Whilst the memories flooded back, I got tired of comparisons, and hoped that in England, I would find an answer to my wandering, restless heart.

Amidst recriminations, Hansi came into my room, with the suggestion that I leave my packing and join her and her husband at

L

dinner in Mayer's Restaurant, which belonged to an ex-racing driver friend of theirs. I agreed and dressed rather frivolously, to cheer myself up.

Henry, (Hansi's husband) gave me a rather startled look from the bottom of the staircase, and I put this down to my colourful attire and immediately thanked him for his invitation to the fancy dress ball.

Hansi burst out laughing as Henry's face became even more perplexed. When he realised that I was teasing him, he sternly reminded both of us to behave ourselves, as he had a certain reputation to uphold as judge in this city. He then took us both by the arm and escorted us to the restaurant amid tittering and laughter from both sides.

As we entered the restaurant, Herr Mayer came forward to greet us personally, but Hansi and I could not keep a straight face. So Henry introduced us saying: "I'm afraid Hans, I've got two potty ladies on my hands, so we shall need a quiet table, to steady them down."

Mayer smiled from ear to ear, his eyes flickering dangerously, as he kissed my hand, for far too long. My companions noticed it too, and Henry waved his finger at Mayer in reprimand! As we sat down, no-one said a word, but I soon became aware that all eyes were on me, just staring. I found this so embarrassing, that I just said the first thing that came into my head, addressing Mayer: "Do you know the song which goes . . . . where have all the flowers gone?"

This was a popular tune of the time and certainly did not deserve the reply I got, which was: "Most of the Austrian flowers have frozen to death, mainly at Stalingrad . . ."

One could have cut the air with a knife, had not Henry intervened, by reminding us that serious conversations were strictly out of bounds, as we had come this evening for a jolly night out. He then turned to Mayer and asked him when his next race was.

He eagerly replied: "At Easter I hope" adding by turning to me, "You have not seen my museum of trophies, wait just one moment while I fetch the key to my study, and I will give you a guided tour."

With that remark, he disappeared, and Hansi whispered into my ear "Just nibble Burgi, don't eat him alive!"

Mayer returned with a bottle of wine, which he opened and placed on the table, then marched me off to his study.

It was a long oblong room, full of cabinets with all kinds of racing mementos. There were also photos of him standing next to some big stars of the screen, like Lillian Harvey, a sweet blonde actress of British background, or one of him with Franziska Gall, whom I had actually met — an artist, oozing with sex appeal. As I was standing there, being shown one famous face after another I wondered what Hansi had worried about. The last thing on his mind was me!

Moments later, however, my idle thoughts were proved wrong, as Mayer stood so close to me that I had nearly no room to breathe. He told me that I was new and exciting, amidst feeble protests from me warning him of my bad track record, married and several times engaged, yet somehow suspended in mid-air.

"I shall rescue you," he said laughingly, and his flashing dark eyes sank into my heart.

I began to be afraid of this swashbuckling fellow, as I could not afford to be hurt by another love affair. It would mean total destruction for me.

Mayer's dynamic personality took over as he asked: "Are you afraid of me because you know we are two of a kind?" He made me face him. "With me everything is black and white," he continued, holding me close as I stared at this handsome man with a sensuous mouth, as he added: "You will be my next woman, to place the Victory Laurel around my neck."

"And then?" I asked. "What then?"

"I will take you into my arms like now, and kiss you in front of the crowd."

"And now . . .?" I wanted to know, but I had hardly finished the words when he kissed me, like a man possessed. I could have kicked myself for letting him just take over like that, without even a murmur, but I had lost control of the whole situation.

When I finally regained my composure I determined, that no matter what he thought, this would remain a brief episode behind closed doors, and nothing more. I justified the whole incident, by telling myself that Hansi was to blame. She had no right to expose me to this kind of temptation. Perhaps she had even done this on purpose to break Major Spreckley and I up for good. After all, she had always considered him far too old for me. Maybe, she was even right, but I could see no possible sense in entering another torrid relationship, especially at this moment in time.

When we returned to the table, it was blatantly obvious what had transpired in that room, as every look from Mayer told its story.

I refused to let Mayer take me home, although the very thought of him, made my heart miss a beat. The chemistry was definitely there, and it was powerful and would under normal circumstances made me curious to explore it further. My head, however, said quite clearly — 'Stop it you little fool, or you will get hurt badly'.

Never one to do what my head told me, but always one to follow my heart, I waved my better intentions goodbye and decided to postpone my trip to England for another week. After all, one week more or less would really make no difference.

I did however begin to feel guilty about Michael Spreckley. To rid myself of this feeling, I telephoned him in the morning. He was delighted to arrange a meeting for the following weekend at his hotel in Bruck a.d. Mur and he suggested that I should get the Binders, who were good friends of mine, to bring me, and that he would take all of us out for dinner.

So after my conversation with Michael, I immediately telephoned them and they happily agreed to the plan as a good meal was always welcome.

The Binders had only recently started to build their own house and had managed via the British authorities to get a licence to open up a petrol station next to it.

When I arrived there the following weekend, so that we could set off together, they eagerly showed me around the building which was still in its early stages. Despite all the difficulties they had done extremely well and I openly admired their hard work. I knew they would make a success of it, because Herr Binder was definitely the best motor mechanic in the area.

When we finally arrived in Bruck, I was glad to see Michael again, if only to get Mayer out of my system. He in turn, was overjoyed to see us all and immediately took us to the Grand Hotel, where we had a good time, but most of all enough food to make our stomachs content.

How prosaic can one get? Food, before romance.

There existed now two worlds within the one country, namely the Austrian one of starvation and hunger, and the British of plenty. They were the Victors . . . . so why should they not have all? To my mind, however, the contrast was too great and Michael agreed with me. He pointed out that the British, would have fought to the last woman or man, and that they would never have surrendered.

We passed the evening discussing this and many other points, when a young officer asked to dance with me, referring to Major Spreckley "With your dad's permission of course". He nearly got his face punched from Michael, which somewhat dampened the high spirits of this lieutenant.

I was relieved when our time was up, and I could head back to Vienna and the judge's home.

Hansi and Henry, handed me a letter, that had arrived while I had been away. The letter was from Mayer and read:

"Dear Burgi,
If you think that you can slip away from me, with a wave of your little hand, you are mistaken. I will never give up. We are two of a kind; we have both fought in the Resistance and we belong together. Until you agree to see me again, I shall be making a nuisance of myself.
Until soon . . . . .
I am yours,
HANS."

What could I do? I sent a message, that I would agree to meet him at his flat the following afternoon. When I arrived there, I told him that I would only stay, if he promised that he would not touch me, but would listen well, until I had finished talking. He could see from my expression that I would not be deterred from my intent, so he agreed.

I began by telling him about my previous weekend with Major Michael Spreckley and continued to give him a full account from A — Z about all the past men in my life, omitting nothing. I told him about the ugly and the enthralling, the glorious and the awful experiences. How in order to survive, I had cheated and lit fires only to extinguish them again, on behalf of freedom, or so I had believed. When I had completed my life story, I then asked him the vital question: "Now that you know everything about me, do you still want to make a nuisance of yourself, because to me this only means one thing, and that is that you want me to become your wife, and that you wish to give me your name after my English divorce?"

His steel-hard face twitched, as he slowly walked towards me. He took me into his arms and replied: "More than ever beloved. I want to make up for what the Nazis, the Gestapo and also the Liberators have done to you." He then kissed me as if there were no tomorrows left for us.

After, what seemed like ages, Hans then began telling me about his life during the war.

The horrors, of having his young brother imprisoned by the Gestapo in Holland and the final decision to blow up that Gestapo H.Q., with everyone in it, knowing that he could do nothing to save his own brother. Cold sweat stood on his forehead as he almost shouted at me: "Why oh why, did it all have to be like this and was it all in vain Burgi?"

I only wished, that I had a comforting answer. But how could I when we were all still licking our wounds which would break open with the cruel memories which time had not yet been able to heal. So I told him that I understood his suffering as someone very dear to me, my mother had died needlessly because she could not get proper medical attention, until it was too late. But I hoped that it had not all been in vain, even though I was very unsure sometimes.

He seemed to forget his own sorrow as he said: "Oh you poor girl, I will make you forget all the bad things in your life and I will erase the memory of every man in your past, so that there will be only you and I, and our love to begin a new future."

Although the picture he painted, appeared serene and harmonious, I could not help but feel torn, by a certain amount of loyalty that I owed Michael, and by the knowledge that the Vienna 'Grand Prix' meant everything to Hans, and that if I agreed to be his wife, I would again have to tremble for the life of a man, I loved.

It seemed that no matter what I decided, the picture of serenity and harmony was far removed from the reality of living.

Yet, underneath it all, I longed for action, a resurrection from the obscurity of my humdrum existence. I knew in my heart that I was a rebel, who wanted and needed the sparks flying high.

When I left Hans Mayer, I pretended that I had no reservations and that I was confident in obtaining my freedom from my British husband on my return to England. He agreed that my going to England was the most efficient way of sorting out my divorce and I left with the promise to return when all was settled.

Unfortunately this meant another confrontation with Major Protheroe, as he was still in charge of handling all the transportation papers which I needed for my journey from Vienna to London. There was no time like the present, I felt; so upon my return to Hansi's and Henry's, I made an appointment for the following day.

Eric received me with icy politeness and made out the relevant documents in front of me. It was in the same office that he handed me my papers, where six months earlier I had asked him to extend my leave of stay, in Vienna. As I gave him my hand to wish him farewell, he pulled it gently towards his lips and said: "Burgi, believe me, a small part of you is still under my skin, and I often recall, when I am sitting alone in this office, the sound of your laughter and that lovely hat, that attracted my attention in the first place." He kissed my hand and we took one last look at each other and I rushed out and down the steps, summoning a taxi to take me home.

"Where to?" the driver asked, and I had to think hard before giving him an answer, as my mind was miles away 'in the only paradise from which we cannot be evicted', that of our memories.

"Gentzgasse 50" I finally replied.

The driver remarked that this was the 'Royal' district.

I simply replied: "Yes indeed, at my aunt's residence, emperors have dined, but I am going there to bid her farewell, as I am leaving for England shortly."

It was now the 1st of March 1948.

The day of my departure from Vienna for my long journey to England had arrived. My family and friends waved me goodbye, as I stood by the window in the train, clutching some flowers and shedding buckets of tears. My aunt was also very distressed as she reminded me over and over again, to write as soon as I got to London. I promised to do so, with the noise of the crowd drowning my parting words . . . . "I will miss you all . . God Bless".

I waved from the window until my relatives and friends were no more than little dots on the platform. Still crying I settled down in my compartment. As I looked around I noted that there were some five British forces' wives or brides also travelling with me. They comforted me and began telling their stories, of how they had met their husbands, enthusiastic about the new land they were travelling to.

Eventually it was my turn, but I was too afraid to tell them the truth, of how I dreaded my arrival in England, as my past was anything but ordinary. However, my companions kept urging me on, asking how Harold and I had met?

I told them the daring tale, of how he had smuggled me into Vienna, under the noses of the Russians. Their mouths, stood wide open in amazement. Pleas for more of this incredible story, for that was what they perceived it to be, brought girls from the next compartment and the next, until there were about twenty or so women all sandwiched either in the corridor and mainly in our small seating area.

An MP patrol came along to see what all the commotion was about, but was sternly told to go away and leave us in peace. He got very angry saying: "What have we got here, some wildcats?" adding, "They will soon tame you in the UK alright."

We all laughed, but when he pushed a pregnant girl out of the way and told her to go back to her own compartment, that was all I needed to see. It was like a red rag to a bull. I got up out of my seat and pushed my way through to him. I took a deep breath and pulled myself up to my full height and called him a bully and added, that I had eaten bigger men than him for breakfast.

He got the message and cleared off to the roaring applause of my companions.

"Please do tell us more of your adventures," they all shouted, and so I did. The air filled with exhilaration as they listened in awe.

As we reached Bruck a.d. Mur, the train suddenly halted, and over the loudspeakers, a voice could be heard, asking for a Mrs Ell to come to the train door! I could hardly believe my ears. It was me that the voice was asking for! The shrieks of the girls confirmed it as they all shouted together: "It's you Burgi!"

As soon as it had sunk in where we had stopped I guessed why! When I looked out of the window, I saw Major Spreckley with a large and very beautiful bouquet of red roses motioning me to come to the door. I hurriedly obeyed.

Although, my companions were half hanging out of the window, Michael took me into his arms and kissed me . . . to the oo's and aaa's of the onlookers. He asked me to send him a telegram, as soon as I arrived, and I promised with the train slowly pulling out of the station.

As the train gained speed, I returned to my compartment, with tears in my eyes. I really was in no mood to continue my story, as memories flooded back of the happy times that Major Spreckley and I had spent. One of the girls noticed my change of mood immediately, and told the others to go back to their compartments, which they readily did.

Sitting there completely enfolded by my thoughts, I wondered about Michael and I. Had he been younger, maybe things would have been different. He was nevertheless a lovely man, one whom I really did not deserve.

I should not have wasted my time on recriminations, as my day of judgement would come soon enough when I reached England and would have to face my husband again. He too had loved me, but had been far too weak for someone like me.

Why? Oh why did I ever marry him? Even though it was too late to cry over spilled milk, I felt sorry for myself because I knew that I would have to pay for my indiscretions, even though I was not wholly to blame. I had no doubt that the circumstances in Austria after the war had not been so bad, I would never have drifted into this marriage. Now I would have to defend my actions in a country that had no idea, what it was like to live under an occupied force.

How had Major Spreckley put it? "One can do almost anything, as long as one does not get caught."

I looked at the lovely roses in front of me on my lap and noticed the card that was pinned to them. I removed the little envelope, placed the roses upon the suitcase on the rack and seated myself to read the enclosed message which said: 'Bon voyage my darling, I will always love you'. Signed 'MICHAEL Your Liberator'.

I kept reading the little note over and over, thinking that Michael had been one of the few to bring me happiness, whilst others had made me into a sinner. Thankfully no-one had managed to penetrate my soul and scar it. It was odd really; in Vienna I had found also passion beyond my wildest dreams and desires, but I had never found the focal point of my life, for which I had fought so hard. That was to find freedom from pressure, from scheming and from pretence, in order to survive. I had finally obeyed my inner rhythm and decided to go forward, but what would I find at my journey's end?

One thing was for certain, there was one more battle to be fought . . . . . . that of freeing myself from a marriage, which had never really existed, between my first Liberator and I, namely between myself and the man who had come to my home in the tiny village of St. Stefan in Austria in 1945, and who without knowing it had changed the entire course of my life.

British Transit Hotel, Astoria

Bloemendaal
4/XII 17

Liebste Burgi,

Sonntag habe ich mein erster Brief
an Dich geschrieben, seitdem ist schon
einiges vorgefallen, worüber ich Dich berichten
muss. Ich bin aber wegen stürmischer
Ereignisse bis jetzt noch nicht dazu
gekommen.

Also ich bin ordnungsgemäss am
Sonntagabend aus London abgefahren. Die
Seereise war eine nichts besonders. Nur
habe ich das "Gewohnheit" ein baar mal in
Halbschlummer für's im Saune gesagt.
Das nur ein bischen Reden hat mich sehr
gefreut gefreut gefehlt

Ich hatte aus London meiner Frau
geschrieben und worüber er auf meine Pläne
was ihr und telegraphiert dass ich Donnerstag
in Zürndrecht sein würde um Alles näher
zu besprechen. Sie war aber eine par Stunde
nach meiner Ankunft in Bloemendaal
am Telephon und ich sie von meiner
Mitte, hörte dass ich schon da war ich
So gleich am Abend noch nach Bloemendaal
gekommen. Da erst unseren anderseits

war also gleich. Sie wollen einer
Scheidung nie zustimmen, und ~~_____~~
des Vorgefallenen zwischen Dir und dem
Arzt her. Das ist natürlich kein Grund
für eine Scheidung, und ich war heut
heute Nachmittag ~~war~~ bei einem alten Dienst-
freund, der Rechts Anwalt ist. Die Sachlage ist
gesetzlich so dass wo sie Dir kein Ehebruch
nachweisen kann, ich meinerseits kein Klage
auf ~~Scheidung~~ ~~bekomme~~ bewilligt ~~—~~ wenn ~~sie~~ sie Ihrerseits
nicht eine Klage wegen meinerseitigen Ehebruch
erheben will. Dann eine Scheidung nicht
ausgesprochen werden. Der Anwalt wird Dir
ein Brief schreiben worin ~~_____~~ er bekanntgibt
dass ich Scheidung bestehe und ~~_____~~ dich
~~_____~~ bittet eine Scheidung zu zustimmen.
Das alles kostet Zeit und unsere privatfinanzielle
Sachen die ich erledigen muss habe ich denn noch
Zwischlosen mit der Firma somit kann ich wie
telegraphiert mit Anfang Jänner bei Dir sein.
Liebes Bessi ich würde sagen du fliegst im
Flugzeug wenn möglich nach England, sonst
könntest du erst im Feber weil wir so immer
unaufschiebbares zu erledigen haben

Ich bin seit ein paar Tages nicht in
Ordnung und habe das Fiebermesser
angelegt. 38° Fieber. Hoffentlich werde
ich nicht Krank weil ich mich sehr
freue möglichst bald bei dir
zu sein. Entschuldige deshalb die
Handschrift heute

Viele Küsse innigst Geliebte

Dein [Unterschrift]

P.S. Die Eltern waren mit einverstanden
[...] ihr habe ich nicht gesagt dass
du Mrs Katt [...] bist...

P.S. Ich schreib bald wieder

Ing.Wilhelm Haberhauer,
Otto u.Walter Kitzinger,
alle Wien,III.,Mohsgasse 4   Wien,den 3.1.1948

Betr.: Beteiligung an unserem Verlag

An

Mrs.Burgi E l l ,
W i e n ,I..
Hotel "ASTORIA"

       Auf Grund unserer vorangegangenen mündlichen Besprechungen
bestätigen wir Ihnen gerne,die mit Ihnen bis jetzt mündlich getroffenen
Vereinbarungen,betreffend Ihre mittätige Beteiligung an unserem Unternehmen unter der Firma

      " Internationale Arbeitsbörse"
     mit internationalem Stellenanzeiger

verbunden mit einer Direktwerbung für eine Arbeitsvermittlung,insbe-
sondere die Vermittlung von Akademikern,nach Übersee.

Der Ordnung halber halten wir diese mündlichen Vereinbarungen nochmals
fest:

1.) Die für das Unternehmen erforderlichen Lizenzen und Genehmigungen
der österreichischen Behörden werden von uns beschafft,bzw.sind
bereits in unseren Händen.Die Eintragung in das Handelsregister
erfolgt mit Beurkundung unseres noch abzuschliessenden endgültigen
Gesellschaftsvertrages.

Die Höhe Ihrer Beteiligung wollen Sie Sich noch vorbehalten; Sie
sind jedoch in Kenntnis,dass Sie keinerlei Bargeld in die Gesell-
schaft einzubringen haben.Es wird Ihnen vielmehr von dem an Sie
auszuzahlenden Gewinnanteilen ein Teilbetrag von den monatlichen
Vorauszahlungen in Abzug gebracht und auf Ihr Kapitalkonto,bis zur
Höhe der von Ihnen übernommenen Stammeinlage gutgeschrieben.

3.) Sie verpflichten Sich Ihre Arbeitskraft in den Dienst des gemein-
samen Unternehmens zu stellen und werden darüber hinaus uns bei
der Beschaffung geeigneter Büroräume weitgehendst behilflich sein.

4.) Alle sonstigen Mittel,insbesondere Barmittel werden ausschliesslich
von uns beigestellt.

5.) Der endgültige Vertrag ist zwischen uns bis zum 15.1.1948 urkundlich
zu errichten.

6.) Wir betrachten diese vorstehende Vereinbarung als rechtsverbindlich
und bitten Sie um Unterschriftsleistung,zum Zeichen Ihres Einverständnisses,auf der Zweitschrift dieses Briefes

Wir freuen uns auf die gemeinsame Arbeit und bleiben mit dem Ausdruck
           der vorzüglichsten Hochachtung

Gedächnis-Protokoll .

Wir haben Ihnen heute ein Anbot betreffend Ihre
Beteiligung an unserem Unternehmen mit zwei Lastkraft-
wagen überreicht.-

Zusätzlich vereinbaren wir ,dass Sie eines der
beiden Lastkraftfahrzeuge in unseren Besitz überschrei-
ben lassen,sobald Sie mit der in der Firma verbleibenden
Teilsumme Ihrer Anteilsquote den Kaufpreis eines der
beiden Wagen zur Abstattung gebracht haben.-

Sie haben uns also dadurch die Möglichkeit gege-
ben einen Wagen bevorzugt zu erwerben;während wir
Ihnen für Ihren Wagen den Kaufpreis zinsenfrei berech-
net haben.- Darüber hinaus haben Sie den Vorzug bis zur
Abzahlung des Ihnen verbleibenden Fahrzeuges ,von beiden
Fahrzeugen 30% des Reingewinnes zu erhalten.-

Zum Zeichen Ihres Einverständnisses wollen Sie
uns bitte die Zweitschrift Ihres Schreibens zurück-
senden.-

Unterschrift: In vorzüglicher Hochachtung :

Pongauer Güter-u.Nah-Fernverkehrs
Transport Ges.m.b.H.

(Ing.Haberhauer)

Wien,am 12.Juni 1947

Karl Spitzweg. (1808—1885)
Kunst und Wissenschaft

Dresdner Fein Papier Erhard Bunkowsky Dresden

E. B. D. Nr. 1456

P Rabe

ERICH ZARTL

BADEN BEI WIEN
HELENENSTRASSE 12
TEL. 852/VI.

WIEN III.
RASUMOFSKYGASSE 7
TEL. U 3857, U 17-8-16

PRÉSIDENCE DE LA RÉPUBLIQUE

REPUBLIQUE FRANÇAISE

0.60 SAINT-LOUIS POSTES

Président de la République

PRÉSIDENCE RÉPUBLIQUE
15-3
196d
PARIS

Madame N.T.A. TILT
8 Moseley Road
KENILWORTH
　　　(Warwickshire)
　　　　　- Grande-Bretagne -

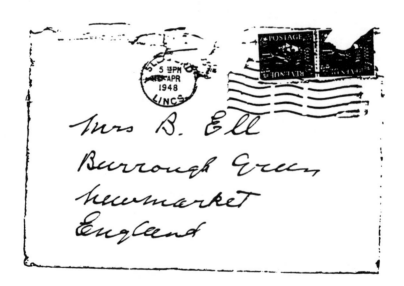